Midsummer 2021

Wittgenstein and Nietzsche Dialogue

Wittgenstein and Nietzsche Dialogue

© Tony Hosking 2021

ISBN 978 09531 08992

Published by The Shogi Foundation
www.shogifoundation.co.uk

First printed in 2021 by CPI Group (UK) Ltd, Croydon, CR0 4YY

Tony Hosking went to Dartington Hall School as a pupil then briefly as a teacher, and graduated in Philosophy and Theology from Balliol College, Oxford. His previous carefully researched and detailed four works *Jalendra and the Tathagata* (2020), *Vishnu-Krishna Shiva-Shakti* (2018), *Shakespeare as Philosopher and the Shakespearean Tragedy of Edward de Vere* (2016), *Oneself the Mystic and Philosopher* (2014), were in turn preceded by writing several very well received books on shogi (Japanese chess). The present work *Wittgenstein and Nietzsche Dialogue* was written over eight months between August 2020 and March 2021 (having been initially substantially researched earlier).

CONTENTS

A Note on the Quotes

A Note on the Quotes

A quote, thankfully, is not inevitably stated out of context, but may be in the right spirit or sense (or senselessness) of the original statement. The text presented here in the main interweaves, to only a very rough chronological extent, quotations from the development of Nietzsche's claimed personal 'interpretations' with quotations from the development of Wittgenstein's objective conceptual descriptions.

The words given here in speech marks, as expressed by Nietzsche as well as Wittgenstein, were written or spoken by them in German – or in Wittgenstein's case sometimes in English (and even at times recorded by his hearers). Originally separate statements made which are linked here are indicated by new speech marks, often given after a '–' (hyphen) directly between speech marks, or instead beginning a new paragraph. On a few occasions the liberty has been taken of condensing particular passages, as indicated (and at times more complete) in the References.

A detailed account of the development of the inspirational works of Wittgenstein and Nietzsche, fully referenced with a comprehensive Bibliography, is given in *Oneself the Mystic and Philosopher* (outlined at the end of this book).

Prologue

Enter Nietzsche and Wittgenstein, meeting Philo.

Philo: "Well, gentlemen, with what cheerful words, made in actions expressing clear and certain free spirit, as recognized by some embodied individual freedom of necessity, shall we three in truth dare begin?"

Nietz: "To stay cheerful when involved in a gloomy and exceedingly responsible business is no inconsiderable art: yet what could be more necessary than cheerfulness? Nothing succeeds in which high spirits play no part".

Witt: "The highest...that I am prepared to carry out is: "to be cheerful in my work"...what lies higher I cannot or do not want to strive for, I can only acknowledge".

Philo: "Why not kindly begin with the first heirs of your inventions, which express completely different essentially ideal kinds of mystical or philosophical spirit?"

Nietz; "The questions as to the beginning of philosophy are quite negligible, for everywhere in the beginning there is the crude, the unformed, the empty and the ugly".

Witt: "Language contains the same traps for everyone...we are still occupied with the same philosophical problems as were the Greeks... because our language has remained the same and keeps seducing us into asking the same questions".

"As little philosophy as I have read, I have certainly not read too little, *rather too much*. I see that whenever I read a philosophical book: it doesn't improve my thoughts at all, it makes them worse". "Reading numbs my soul". Yet "I believe it might interest a philosopher, one who can think himself, to read my notes. For even if I have hit the mark only rarely, he would recognize what targets I had been ceaselessly aiming at".

Nietz: "I know my fate". "*Beyond Good and Evil* [for example]... People will *dare* read it, I suppose, some time around the year 2000".

Philo: "Please each, in turn, be so kind as to give a brief account of your first such book, with as much detail as deemed necessary – after which we will all give our main comments, even critical evaluations – although I feel sure that each of you is the best critic of your own first work. And do we agree that instinctive ancient age of tragedy comes before more abstract beauty, austere rational forms of logic?"

Wittgenstein and Nietzsche together happily smiled in some outwardly silent complete agreement.

The Birth of Tragedy
out of the Spirit of Music

Nietz: "I shall fix my gaze on those two artistic deities of the Greeks, Apollo and Dionysus...representations of *two* worlds of art, utterly different". In concert "the two gods of art...is a tremendous opposition... to beget...Attic tragedy".

The Birth of Tragedy – "what an *impossible* book had to grow out of a task so unfavourable to youth!" – "with this questionable book, my instinct...turned *against* morality and invented a fundamentally opposite doctrine and valuation of life, purely artistic...I called it the *Dionysian*".

Philo: "– rather than Apolline, or both".

Nietz: "I was concerned with nothing except to guess why precisely Greek Apollinianism had to grow out of a Dionysian subsoil". *The Birth of Tragedy out of the Spirit of Music* – that means the "Dionysian art of music" – "*tragedy arose from the tragic chorus...the Greek satyr chorus...of myth and ritual*". "Later, the attempt is made to show the god as real, and to represent the visionary form...this is the beginning of the 'drama'".

"The satyr...this man of the woods...still unaffected by knowledge... [and] culture...[is] the archetype of man...an inspired reveller...the true man...goat-like satyrs...[each] musician, poet, [hooved] dancer". "Singing and dancing, man expresses himself as a member of a higher community" – even "the Dionysian...mystical sense of Unity".

Philo: "If I may add a little to this here: the cult of Dionysus swept across Greece during the seventh and sixth centuries BC. Following the invention circa 625 BC of the dithyramb, that is, choral song honouring Dionysus, the rise and fall of Dionysian drama spanned just over three hundred years; reaching its zenith with the great Attic dramatists of the fifth century, centred at the theatre of Dionysus in Athens. Tragedy was entirely choral until Thespis arrived with his Dionysian chorus in Athens circa 534 BC, and introduced the prologue as well as speeches, with which staging the drama really begins".

"I have to say that your early 'purely artistic' and 'higher' view already sounds not only artistic but also involving religious and moral evaluation. Yet forgive me: pray – or rather please – continue".

Nietz: "I should believe only in a God who understood how to dance".

The Birth of Tragedy proclaims that the "phenomena we are...[is] an illusion...a continuous becoming in time...If we look away from our own ["waking"] 'reality'...if we see our empirical existence...as an idea of ["its substratum"] the primal Oneness...then we must see the dream as the *illusion of illusion*" – with "Apollo, the interpreter of dreams".

Yet: "Only as an aesthetic phenomenon is the world and the existence of man eternally justified" – "beauty triumphs over the suffering inherent in life".

In my first book, "art – and *not* morality – is presented as the properly [or "actual", *eigentliche*] *metaphysical* activity". In "longing for the primal and the natural", that is, "longing for...redemption by illusion...I [did] feel compelled to make the metaphysical assumption that the Truly Existent, the primal Oneness [Dionysus], eternally suffering ["entirely thoughtless"] and contradictory, also needs the delightful vision, the pleasurable illusion [of art] for its constant redemption:...we behold...their reciprocal necessity...the whole world of torment is necessary so that the individual can create the redeeming vision" – "floating in the purest bliss and painless contemplation...of it...peacefully" – "in...the aesthetic, purely contemplative will-less ["Apolline"] state...given that the will is precisely that which is not aesthetic" – "and we might even describe Apollo as...the *principium individuationis* [principle of individuation]".

"Dionysian...will...[means] the eternal life that lies beyond the phenomenal world...the eternal life of the will...'We believe in eternal life' is tragedy's cry" – "join the Dionysian procession from India to Greece!" "Here, in the highest artistic symbolism, we behold...the terrible wisdom of Silenus": "The best of all things is something entirely outside your grasp: not to be born, not to *be*".

Nietzsche then fell silent.

Witt: "In art it is hard to say anything as good as: saying nothing".

Philo: "– or just saying 'beautiful'".

Witt: "And the beautiful is what makes happy".

Philo: "As there is nothing ever objectively – or strictly speaking even morally – wrong to be put right in or about art as such".

Witt: When we "have no criterion of correctness...we can't talk about 'right'".

Nietz: "But all life is dispute over taste and tasting!"

Philo: "Thus speaks the inspired artist directed by personal morality; striving for a most noble, higher, elevated taste. There is fine taste, good taste, bad taste and the tasteless, corrupt taste – worse than no taste at all! Sublimely beautiful art is rare, for art allows so much bad even ugly art".

Nietz: "Because...most of us are bad poets. The aesthetic phenomenon is fundamentally a simple one: grant someone only the ability continually to see a living play, to live constantly surrounded by hordes of spirits, and he will be a poet...Enchantment is the precondition of all dramatic art".

Philo: "To enter the poetic world requires personal enchantment (one might perhaps say that's the en-trance-meant!); passionate commitment of aesthetic interpretation, allows a person to be joyfully moved, uplifted, inspired, seized, captivated by a fascinating, delightful beauty. But are we all living only poetically, of 'such stuff as dreams are made'?"

Witt: "I cannot seriously suppose that I am at this moment dreaming" – "if I am dreaming...it is also being dreamed that these words have any meaning".

Philo: "Most certainly, all the world could not be the sleeper's dream, for meaningful dream presupposes real and certain meaning of its words.

(facing Nietzsche) "Artistic enchantment, aesthetic belief as personal reality, suspends perception of objective and moral reality. Yet a dream is only recognized as such after re-awakening, compared to waking reality – even if, as you say, one calls out while dreaming: 'It is a dream! I want to dream on!'"

Nietz: I wrote of "the Greeks, who revealed the profound mysteries of their artistic doctrines...not in concepts but in the vividly clear forms of their...two gods of art, Apollo and Dionysus".

Witt: I too once wrote: "There is, indeed, the inexpressible [or "that which cannot be put into words"; *Unaussprechliches*]. This shows itself; it is the mystical".

Philo: "Any doctrine, or even overwhelming mystical feeling, indeed any kind of meaning at all, as so called is essentially conceptual".

Nietz: "the *mystery doctrine of tragedy*: [communicates] the basic understanding of the Unity of all things, individuation seen as the primal source of evil, art as the joyful hope that the spell of individuation can be broken, as a presentiment of a restored Oneness" – "in tragedy...Dionysus speaks the language of Apollo, but Apollo finally speaks the language of Dionysus, and thus is attained the supreme goal of tragedy and of art".

Philo: "If speaking no more, then Dionysus sings of beautiful illusory Apolline interpretation, and Apollo sings of Dionysian tragic wisdom!"

Nietz: "How I now regret that I did not...permit myself *a new language* ...that I toiled with Schopenhauerian and Kantian formulae to express strange and new valuations fundamentally opposed to [theirs]...I... obscured and spoiled Dionysian new valuations" – "beneath the heaviness and dialectical joylessness" – "*The Birth of Tragedy*...smells offensively Hegelian...An 'idea' – the antithesis Dionysian and Apollonian...in tragedy this antithesis elevated to a unity".

Philo: "The main source of conceptual illusion is to idealize by over-simplification. The trouble with all philosophers renowned as influential system-builders, including Kant and Hegel, is that they are too simple! For instance, dialectical opposition of identities (thesis and antithesis) makes another identity (synthesis); but taking concepts as only dialectical falsely, unrealizably, reduces difference to claimed necessary negation, opposition then non-self-contradiction. Difference is other than only contradictory. And this is other than merely in opposition to dialectics!

"In describing Apollo as the divine principle of individualization, so that the individual can create and contemplate the redeeming vision, in order to 'sit peacefully in his tossing boat amid the waves' of the world, you explicitly recognized as Apolline what Schopenhauer had said of the illusory egocentric Indian 'veil of Maya. Just as the boatman sits in his small boat, trusting his frail craft in a stormy sea...rising and falling with the howling, mountainous waves, so in the midst of a world full of suffering and misery the individual man calmly sits, supported by and trusting the *principium individuationis*'".

Nietz: And once more, "Dionysian...will...[means] the eternal life that lies beyond the phenomenal world".

Philo: "So in *The Birth of Tragedy* you were tragically misguided by the representational metaphysics of Kant, Schopenhauer and Hegelian dialectics. Kantian noumena (essence behind apparent phenomena) is identified by Schopenhauer – through Indian mysticism and Platonic Ideas – as Will, and One Absolute Will you identified as Dionysian".

Witt: When composing my first book, I also wrote, "I cannot bend the happenings of the world to my will...completely". Thus: "The world is independent of my will". Yet I too believed "There is really only one world soul". "And in this sense I can also speak of a will that is common to the whole world...As my idea is the world[-idea], in the same way my will is the world-will".

Philo: "From such words I understand that each of you read – and to some youthful eager but rash extent accepted – Schopenhauer's *The World as Will and Representation* (or *Idea*); which most heavily and uncritically draws upon the metaphysics of not only Kant's representational philosophy but also Indian teachings of will and selflessness".

Witt: I further wrote: "Aesthetically, the miracle is that the world exists". "Not how the world is, is the mystical, but that it is. The contemplation of the world *sub specie aeterni* [under eternal form]...[and] feeling of the world as a limited whole is the mystical".

Nietz: "Apollo I [did] see as...the sole path to true Redemption through illusion. While in the mystical...Dionysus the spell of individuation is broken".

Philo: "Apollo dreams, casting the illusory veil of individuality, heroic will, beautiful forms of sculpture, painting and poetry; in dynamic so-called opposition to Dionysian ecstatic, overwhelming enrapture in music, the chorus – together creating the art of tragedy.

"Yet such art is always recognized, so called as a cultural and personal expression, enhancing Nature as itself unaesthetic objectivity. Once more, any aesthetic perception of natural beauty relatively completely suspends perception of Nature as objective. Birds, for example, sing and display dancing. But it has to be said that the uncultural 'poet', as further claimed of the satyr, expresses senseless confusion. For the world of individuals as poetic is claimed as Apolline dream, interpretation. Again, when anyone asserts or attributes instinct, feeling or passion that means essentially as culturally, conceptually called, even if 'the highest artistic symbolism'".

Nietz: Subsequently I wrote of the *"Apollinian – Dionysian...antithesis ...[of] artistic powers...[as]: dream...vision...poetry; [and] intoxication... passion, song, dance"*.

Philo: *"The Birth of Tragedy* distinguishes between the primal One, the natural satyr as uncultural archetypal true poetic man and human culture. But the natural – or mythical believed – world of the horse-tailed and hooved satyrs, lustfully pursuing maenads (bacchants) and nymphs running barefoot in the woods, is judged as in the world of illusion too! Surely the wild satyr would perceive the dramatic satyr chorus to be just as 'timidly...[like] a dainty, flute-playing, sentimental shepherd!' Yet still the satyrs, together in a chorus as one, most joyfully understand, believe their participating in the world to be illusion; ecstatically singing of the mystery doctrine of tragedy that all appearance is eternally One".

Nietz: That "life is at bottom indestructibly powerful and joyful, is given concrete form as a satyr chorus, a chorus of natural beings, living ...remaining the same for ever". *"Dionysus* of the Greeks [means]: the religious affirmation of life, life whole and not denied or in part" – "in...eternity...in Dionysian ecstasy...we are happy to be alive, not as [Apolline] individuals but as *the* single Living thing, merged with its creative delight". "The individual must be consecrated to something higher than himself – that is the meaning of tragedy...all the ennoblement of mankind is enclosed in this supreme task". Thus the call sounded out: "sacrifice with me in the temple of both deities!"

Philo: "Such mystical self-sacrifice, of suffering embodied individual temporal life, would abolish every individual will for eternal Life of One Will. The satyr chorus hopes not merely to be at One with Dionysus, but for all individuality dissolved as the One selfless Dionysus!"

Nietz: I even wrote: "beyond the phenomenal world, regardless of all destruction...the eternal Life of the [Dionysian] Will is left untouched".

Philo: "In other words, Apollo dreams, ever asleep to the selfless, absolutely completely Untouched, Dionysian Original Reality; and Redemption is proclaimed as Absolute yet endlessly repeated Goal and not the mere way of Apolline art as double illusion. But any claim to Being Alone without the world is senseless, for that would exclude its very words, actually stated, including of any mystical merging.

"Further, such so-called tragic Dionysian wisdom, even death or other-worldliness, does not overcome becoming – for that is the very cause involved in creating, perpetuating the world of becoming. How could all apparent illusion be overcome by further illusion? How can new wood ever put out the fire?"

Nietz: Indeed I later wrote, "Dionysus cut to pieces is a *promise* of life: it will be eternally reborn and return again from destruction".

Witt: "The temporal immortality of the human soul...this assumption... Is this eternal life not as enigmatic as our present one?"

Nietz: Again, "the illusion of illusion...is the reflection of eternal, primal suffering, the sole foundation of the world: 'illusion' here is the reflection of the eternal contradiction".

Philo: "Apollo as god of all individual creation and destruction, every apparent person and thing, every word, affirmation and denial, would have to include each self-contradiction as Apolline illusion. Accordingly, Dionysus essentially seems Apolline, self-contradictory and illusory, even when called the Absolute Selfless, Non-Apolline, One Life: absolutely completely 'selfless' yet fated to appear as individual self, endlessly reborn as the tragic god of art, precisely opposing all Apolline art.

"Once more, your dialectical opposition between Apollo and Dionysus is too clear-cut, excessively Apolline. Recognizing an essential difference between, on the one hand, reason, contemplation, vision, poetry, and on the other hand, passion, intoxication, music, dance, is actually relatively merged, that is, other than absolutely sharp exclusion".

Nietz: I later also wrote of "The misunderstanding of [Dionysian] passion and [Apolline] reason, as if the latter were an independent entity ...and as if every passion did not possess its quantum of reason". Thus there must arise the Apolline "vision of the most afflicted ["suffering"], contrary, contradictory being [Dionysus], who can find redemption and deliverance only in *illusion*".

Philo: "And so I understand that Apollo desires and needs Freedom, from apparent individual suffering, in the blissful Dionysian music of One Reality, while Dionysus desires and needs the beautiful artistic dream of Apollo, to appear identified, to arise as individual Dionysus; and only together do the two gods of art express tragic music-drama.

"The satyr chorus, joyous in both creation and destruction, ecstatically sings of the mystery of birth, life and death as the appearance of the evil spell of Apolline individuality – including of satyrs and Dionysus – that is believed not only hopefully can but inescapably will be broken to 'restore' eternal Dionysian Life as One, underlying the endless cycle of rebirth – as in a similar divine way enacted by Shiva dancing in India. Dionysus appears fatefully torn to pieces (also like Osiris scattered in Egypt) as individual and One. The Dionysian Oneness, even as chorus, repeatedly fragments itself, needing to appear individualized, endlessly desiring art as double illusion. In proclaimed purely poetic reflective symbolism of entirely actionless, will-less Apolline bliss, the two gods together allow contemplation of perpetual Redemption from suffering, in both art as double illusion and One Reality. The triumph of art over suffering life is fleeting and yet eternal. The Fate of every arising suffering individual is blissful Dionysian Oneness, underlying endless illusory tragic rebirth!"

Nietz: "life is something essentially amoral...valueless in itself". Amidst "nature's cruelty...the terrible truth...the horror and absurdity of existence...there approaches a redeeming, healing enchantress – *art*".

Philo: "Or *The Birth of Tragedy* is for artists glorifying two gods of tragic art – yet still no Greek goddess of art as such looks them in the eye. And again, this claimed 'purely artistic' work is within the context of art, mystical religion and morality. Faith in creating art 'in the highest artistic symbolism' is also moral; likewise when Nature is judged to be cruel. And as observed at the outset, the Apolline dream world of aesthetic interpretation always suspends, that is, can never admit any objectivity or morality as such. The impersonal itself as so called, evaluated, is not meaningless but objective. Nature or life relatively in itself as objective is completely amoral, unaesthetic and unreligious".

Nietz: "poetry...wishes to be...the unadorned expression of truth...The contrast [is] between this authentic, natural truth and the lie [or "falsity"] of culture".

Witt: While composing my first book I also noted down: "Wishing is not acting, but willing is acting...The wish precedes the event, the will accompanies it". "The will seems always to have to relate to an idea...The act of will is not the cause of the action but is the action itself...willing is acting. One cannot will without acting".

Philo: "The artistic wish to be unadorned, uncultural, overlooks that all truth, including all poetic truth, the natural and any cult – even Dionysian – is so called by some rational cultural statement actually made".

Nietz: "the entire [first] book knows only one...meaning behind all events...an...amoral artist-god...creating and destroying...doing both good and ill" – at times even acting as "a cruel, savage daemon".

Philo: "That means Dionysus is not One as amoral, but arises as dual: both moral and immoral, divine and demonic! Again, Dionysus too needs to be repeatedly created, reborn as individual. For each and every person, the claimed constantly repeated redemption from the so-called illusory world of suffering individuality is only through the symbolism of Apollo's art as double illusion".

Nietz: "Dionysian release from the fetters of individuation" means "a mystical sense of Unity" – "mystical...Being". And later I wrote down: "The word '*Dionysian*' means: an urge to Unity, a reaching out beyond personality, the everyday...an ecstatic affirmation of the total character of life as that which remains the same, just as powerful, just as blissful, through all change; the great pantheistic sharing of joy and sorrow...the feeling of the necessary unity of creation and destruction".

Witt: "No sign leads us beyond itself".

Philo: "By that I understand that no word points absolutely completely beyond its linguistic world".

Nietz: *The Birth of Tragedy* asserts that "symbolism of music cannot be exhaustively interpreted through language, because it symbolically refers to the...contradiction and...suffering within the primal Oneness... beyond and prior to all phenomena".

Philo: "Not everything is merely words, but as already stated, every meaning, including mystical feeling or doctrine, is so called by rational conceptual kind of language. And indeed, Dionysian laughing delight at the tragic birth and inevitable death of every wilful individual – even the most heroic – claims the very word of artistic double "illusion' here is the reflection of the eternal contradiction', that is, able to point to uncreated and so indestructible power of eternal entirely selfless Dionysian Will. In Apolline symbols, the primal Oneness is called beyond and prior to, underlying, the phenomenal world of creation and destruction of all individual appearances, and all thought; and the expression 'that which remains the same' is quintessential Apolline symbolism!

"The proclaimed artistic opposition is between Apolline 'illusion...as a continuous becoming in time' of creation and destruction, against eternal 'Dionysian Reality' of selfless 'Being', as 'the Truly Existent, the primal Oneness', 'the One Real Dionysus'. And you said that in *The Birth of Tragedy* you 'obscured and spoiled Dionysian new valuations' – but they are against life, condemning all life as in time and so illusory evil spell of bondage! Following old Silenus, foster-father of Dionysus, drunkenly crying out the moral judgment that "The best is not to be", Dionysian so-called wisdom calls for complete selflessness, self-sacrifice: for the Apolline beautiful dream world of art too is fleeting part of suffering the selfish world of so-called mere appearances. Our whole waking everyday reality is condemned as only suffering dream, compared to 'looking away' – even from the illusory path in 'the highest artistic symbolism' – for the Absolute Goal of Redemption, Oneness Beyond".

Nietz: "tragedies have to do with precisely what is incurable... inescapable". I later wrote on "*the tragic*. The Greeks...misunderstood it ...Yearning for nothingness is a *denial* of tragic wisdom, its opposite!" I further wrote of "Aristotle's great misunderstanding...that one is 'purged'" of "two *depressive* affects, terror and pity...through their arousal...[by] tragedy...Tragedy would then signify...the instinct for life destroying itself...decline [and "resignation"]...[But instead] tragedy is a *tonic*".

Philo: "Dionysus cut to pieces promises endless rebirth. However, the tragic so-called wisdom of intoxicated Silenus, refusing wilfully to advance, exemplifies self-destructive desire of the weak individual not to 'find' and improve oneself but to lose oneself.

"So in 'precocious' youth, you followed Schopenhauer and unsparing Indian ascetics in misunderstanding tragic fate too – only later keenly recognizing that wilful noble individuals abandon any tragic sentiment of resignation! Willing creates and destroys, so liberates or enslaves".

Witt: I also wrote down: "I will call 'will' first and foremost the bearer of good and evil". "What is good and evil is essentially the I, not the world". "Good and evil only enter through the subject...It would be possible to say (á la Schopenhauer): It is not the world of Idea that is either good or evil; but the willing subject...Here [however] the nature of the subject is completely veiled".

Philo: "Perverse ascetics will to deny, eliminate individual will, which shows cowardly aversion, fear and hatred of fleeting happiness, reason, self and all life, yearning to cease suffering change. In great contrast, unsuppressed individual freewill shows commanding strength of self-determination, a will to some complete independence".

Nietz: Later on I thought: "'*Apollinian*' means: the urge to perfect self-sufficiency, to the typical 'individual', to all that simplifies, ["measures",] distinguishes, makes strong, clear...: freedom under the law [afterwards: "submission to rule and concept"]...the highest form of self-affirmation in a cool, noble, severe beauty: the Apollinianism of the Hellenic will". But: "Alas, my friends, we must overcome even the Greeks!"

Philo: "So your later tragic wisdom of – not selflessness, even of One Will – but noble individual will, turning suffering life to one's advantage, would be even more appropriately called Apolline rather than Dionysian!"

Nietz: "Dionysus is a philosopher".

Philo: "– of claimed Apolline interpretation! But here I should not leap ahead of your first book, about which I would like to express a little more.

"You wrote of the Dionysian man 'who runs the risk of longing for a Buddha-like denial of the will [and 'yearning for the Void']. He is saved by art...But when...everyday reality [is artless], it becomes repellent; this leads to a mood of asceticism, of denial of the will...for...action can change nothing...Understanding kills action, action depends on a veil of illusion...True understanding, insight into the terrible truth ['nature's cruelty...the horror and absurdity of existence'], outweighs every motive for action...[Artless] an immortal 'Beyond' is denied'. Your vision, again following Schopenhauer and many Indian mystics, darkly divines the will as the source of all suffering, and further would subdue, deny all willing in 'the aesthetic, purely contemplative will-less state'. Poetic reflective symbolism is claimed as completely actionless, will-less, double illusion – alone justifying life eternally: Redeeming, Liberating. But it needs to be recognized that poetic interpretation is actually never will-less. *The Birth of Tragedy* ignores all real will required to interpret any personal value, including will to create and contemplate art.

"In your book I see that, despite the universal denunciation of culture, art is not yet emphasized explicitly as error (*Irrthümer*) or lie (*Lüge*), but called the illusion (*Schein*) of illusion: meaning merely apparent double individual 'reflection', which is the representation of representation of One Dionysian Reality. Nevertheless, illusion essentially means unreality, untruth, falsity in the sense of objectively acting under some unreal kind of perception, error or mistake; one can likewise speak of misconception, misapprehension, delusion, deceptive appearance, pretence, make-believe, imitation, fantasy, figments of imagination.

10

"An aesthetic experience is always believed to be real or true, or even falsity, as personal. To call this unobjective art an illusion is to condemn personal reality as unreal, mistaken, even lie – that signifies, objectively certainly, not only complete disenchantment with art but a real blunder! To take subjective art as the means, the doubly illusory means, to deny all real life is a great double misunderstanding. For as made clear earlier, the Apolline dream world of only aesthetic interpretation is never able to recognize any objectivity or morality as such. Art as personal art is never actually compared to perception of objective or moral reality.

"Accordingly no one can ever rightly, correctly, justly or decently, say that the poetic artist lives a lie, lives in error, lives in an illusion; or that the poet when making no claim to objectivity – as never able to do so genuinely – fails to admit any objectivity. But the poet who makes claims to objectivity must fail, must be in error. For all error or correctness is objective. And, it may be added, philosophy compares different kinds of practices only conceptually, as will assuredly be made more explicit in due course.

"Once more, *The Birth of Tragedy* affirms Dionysus and Apollo as necessarily 'within the context of' each other. Compared to One Dionysian Reality, life is condemned as merely illusion; and double illusory poetic interpretation even sees science as nothing but interpretation. Anyone can certainly take the Dionysian and Apolline as personal belief in the Higher, or as divinely commanding. However, you proclaimed not only an artistic but also a moral and mystical belief denying all genuine objective reality! Such excessive kind of judgment mistakenly claims to place everything in the context of artistic symbolism and Oneness".

Nietz: *The Birth of Tragedy* has "the task...*to see science under the lens of the artist, but art under the lens of [One] life*" – and still "the book... [is] presented within the context of *art*". For again: "Only as an aesthetic phenomenon is the world and the existence of man eternally justified".

Witt: Reasons in aesthetics are "further descriptions".

Nietz: "again...I find...[my] book...embarrassing...confused...so sure of its convictions that it is above any need for proof...a book for initiates".

Witt: A man's religious "unshakeable belief...will show, not by reasoning or by appeal to ordinary grounds for belief, but rather by regulating for all in his life".

Philo: "Most certainly, proof is not needed, and indeed not possible, when appealing to one's sense of objectively unjustifiable, unscientific meanings. And Redemption can only ever be needed as personal".

Nietz: I later wrote of "the older Hellenic instinct...the Dionysian... triumphant Yes to life beyond death and change; *true* life as collective continuation of life through procreation, through the mysteries of sexuality [and "the orgy"]...*to realize in oneself* the eternal joy of becoming".

Philo (facing Nietzsche): "The cult of Dionysus spread over Greece from the seventh century BC; the satyr chorus ecstatically proclaiming Life is eternally One. This belief affirms the Dionysian herd as selfless: sacrificing and ultimately devoid of all individual concerns – judged as only endless Apolline illusory rebirth. Your subsequent 'tragic wisdom', however, would recognize the oppression of traditional herd morality demanding selfless obedience for the sake of that herd. But, at first, your instinct and reason mistook traditional morality for all 'morality...[as] a 'will to the denial of life', a secret instinct of annihilation'; against which you invented a too combative, too simple, dialectical, so-called 'purely artistic' Dionysian view, claiming to oppose all morality, whether of a group or individual. But again your early view is also guided by morality; condemning everything of this temporal life for a so-called better, eternal, Dionysian selfless Unity Beyond".

Nietz: Later too I wrote down: "'Eternal bliss': psychological nonsense. Brave and creative men *never* consider pleasure and pain as ultimate ["eternal"] values...one must *desire* both if one is to achieve anything".

Philo: "Absolute Bliss, even though essentially unrealizable, senseless, can be personal belief. And real personal belief never genuinely claims to deny all life, nor judges the whole world as error.

"You critically wrote of *The Birth of Tragedy*: 'Truly, nothing could be more opposed to the purely aesthetic interpretation and justification of the world as taught in this book...than...moral...absolute Standards...which relegates art, *all* art to the realm of *falsehood* – it denies, condemns and damns it. In this...I had always sensed...*hostility to life*...disgust and antipathy for life, merely disguised...as the belief in an 'other' or a 'better' ["transcendental"] life. Hatred of the 'world'...a yearning for non-existence...a 'will to decline'...a sign of...exhaustion...life *must* constantly and inevitably be in the wrong'. It has to be said that these words of total condemnation – which you aimed at traditional, in particular Christian, morality – when taken in both a moral and a specifically objective sense, express twofold right criticism of Dionysian absolutely selfless Oneness expressed in *The Birth of Tragedy*, and any still held view of all the world, including art, as illusion or error!"

Nietz: "a youthful work...a 'first book'...how disagreeable it seems to me now".

Nietz: "I contend that there has never been a philosopher who did not finally look down on the philosophy he invented in his youth with disdain [or "contempt"], or at least suspicion".

Witt: "I don't believe I have ever invented a line of thinking. I have always taken one over from someone else...for my work of clarification. That is how...Schopenhauer, Frege, Russell...have influenced me" – although "in Norway during the year 1913-14 I had some thoughts of my own".

Philo: "By that I understand you to mean when beginning to write your invented idealism of logically atomic picturing and unsayable showing of the *Tractatus*".

Nietz: "Our usual...observation...imagines...an empty space ["between ...facts"], it *isolates* every fact. In reality, however, all our doing and knowing is not a succession of facts and empty spaces but a continuous flux [later: "indivisible flowing"]. Now, belief in freedom of will [later: "that is to say in *identical* facts and in *isolated* facts"] presupposes ["erroneously"] that *every individual action is isolate and indivisible*; it is an *atomism* in the domain of willing and knowing...[a] false presupposition...Through words and concepts we are still continually misled into imagining things as being simpler than they are, separate from one another, indivisible, each existing in and for itself. A philosophical mythology lies concealed in *language*".

Philo (turning to Wittgenstein): "That signals, or anticipates, your turn!"

Witt: "An entire mythology is laid down in our language". "People are deeply embedded [later: "caught up"] in philosophical, i.e. grammatical confusions. And to free them from these..." – "We must plough through the whole of language".

Nietz: "As is so often the case, the unity of the word does not guarantee the unity of the thing".

Witt: Indeed: "Our language is constructed on an apparently simple scheme, so that we are inclined to look at language as being much simpler than it is".

Philo: "– which then was taken to its most general logical extreme".

Witt: When composing my first book, I also noted: "Don't get involved in partial problems, but always take flight to where there is a free view over the whole single great problem". For at first I did assume: "The great problem round which everything that I write turns is...the world a priori".

Philo: "I understand the Latin expression *a priori*, that literally means 'from prior', as a most strict reasoning means logical following, that is, deduction or inference, of universal necessity from and in complete principle. But again, please continue without my interruption".

Witt: The *Tractatus Logico-Philosophicus* – "I finished the book in August 1918". "When I wrote that, I had Plato's idea of finding the general idea lying behind all particular meanings of a word".

I assumed: "The simplest proposition, the elementary proposition, asserts the existence of an atomic fact". "The propositions which represent this ultimate [irreducible] connexion of terms I call[ed too], after B. Russell, atomic propositions". For example, I affirmed: "the understanding of general propositions obviously depends on that of atomic propositions".

And clearly: "none of our experience is a priori...All that we can [so] describe at all could also be otherwise". "There are no necessary facts; all facts are contingent...of experience...No fact can be necessary, for if it has sense to affirm it, it also has sense to deny it...The negation of a proposition [of experience] must have sense".

"Philosophical problems are not solved by experience [as such], for what we talk about in philosophy are not [directly contingent] facts" – "existence and non-existence...means *facts*, not [essential] concepts".

But I reasoned: "It is the essence of philosophy not to depend on experience...philosophy is *a priori*". "The object [or "aim", *Der Zweck*] of philosophy is ["essentially"] the logical clarification of thoughts...to make propositions clear"– "as always, the a priori certain proves to be something purely logical". "Logic must take care of itself". "Logic is prior to every experience – that something is so" – "logic is a priori". "Logic is not a theory but a reflection of the world". Thus I envisaged "the all-embracing world-mirroring logic...the great mirror".

My early logical representational view can be essentially, very briefly, sketched as follows. "A proposition is [only] a description of fact...and is either true or false". "To understand a proposition means to know what is the case, if it is true...without knowing whether it is true". "A proposition ...is a picture" – of realizable "positive...[or] negative fact". "A picture contains the possibility of the situation that it represents". "A logical picture of facts is a thought". Further: "Propositions...cannot represent what they must have in common with reality in order to be able to represent it – the logical form...this mirrors itself...propositions *show* the logical form of reality" – "we know a priori the possibility of a logical form". "A picture can represent every reality whose form it has...A picture, however, cannot represent its form of representation; it shows it forth" – and that means: "A proposition shows its sense".

Accordingly: "My propositions are elucidatory in this way: he who understands me finally recognizes them as nonsensical (*unsinnig*), when he has climbed out through them, on them, over them. (He must so to speak throw away the ladder, after he has climbed up on it.) He must surmount [or "overcome", *überwinden*] these propositions; then he sees the world rightly".

"What is essential...cannot be said". "What can be shown cannot be said". And again, "the inexpressible...shows itself; it is the mystical". I ended the *Tractatus* with the words: "Whereof one cannot speak, thereof one must be silent".

Wittgenstein then became silent.

Nietz: So too my statements: "For me they were steps. I have climbed up upon them – therefore I had to pass over them. But they thought I wanted to settle down on them" – and "in certain cases, as the [medieval] saying suggests, one *remains* a philosopher only by – being silent".

Witt: "the point of the book is ethical...My work consists of two parts: the one presented here, and all that I have not written. And precisely this second part is the important one...All of that which many others today are just babbling, I have firmly set in place in my book by remaining silent about it". And in its Preface I wrote: "the truth of the thoughts that are here set forth seems to me unassailable and definitive. I am, therefore, of the opinion that the problems [of philosophy] have in essentials been finally solved". I later clarified: "On all [philosophical] questions we discuss I have no opinion".

Philo: "That mixture of somewhat guarded uncertainty, and yet still complete certainty, also overlooks that thinking never settles anything. And the ever unsayable so called surely expresses self-contradiction, self-contempt of reason. Even so, I understand that, on completion of the *Tractatus*, you duly left the philosophical stage for just over a decade".

Witt: On my eventual return, in defence of the *Tractatus*, I maintained that "no language is conceivable [or "thinkable", *denkbar*] which does not represent this world". "Grammar is a mirror of reality". "Grammar is not the expression of what is the case but of what is possible".

Philo: "This, then, marks a shift of emphasis from logic towards grammar, as essential conceptual rules of language".

Witt: "Grammar is a description of language". "No description...can justify the rules of language". "You cannot justify grammar. For such a justification would have to be...a description of the world...[that] might be otherwise, and the propositions expressing this different description would have to be false. But grammar requires them to be senseless".

Philo: "In other words, contingent experiential truth or falsity is never necessary conceptual truth or falsity. Grammar describes what conceptually must be possible, sense, or impossible, senseless".

Witt: I still then held: "Language is connected with reality by picturing it, but that [essential] connection cannot be...explained". But "I have been forced to recognize grave mistakes in what I wrote in that first book".

Philo: "If I may ask: what, then, did you need to do?"

15

Witt: I had to "plunge into something terrible" to "put straight", "put correctly", having been "misled" by the expressions "sense" and "nonsense".

Nietz: "Nothing is rarer among philosophers than *intellectual integrity*".

Witt: "It is characteristic of obsessions that they are not recognized... The problems [in the philosophical tradition] do not appear to concern questions about language but rather questions of fact of which we do not yet know enough. It is for this reason that...you expect ["information"]... a theory...of a science called metaphysics".

Nietz: "Scientific philosophy has to be very careful about smuggling in errors".

Witt: "the pretence is that philosophy is some sort of science. People speak of it almost as they might speak of medicine" – as I even did on later occasion, as when remarking: "The philosopher is a man who has to cure himself of many sicknesses of the understanding". And: "There is not *a* philosophical method, though there are indeed methods, like different therapies".

Philo: "Philosophers mistakenly expect and seek new knowledge of experience".

Nietz: Again, in *The Birth of Tragedy*, "art...is presented as the properly *metaphysical* activity".

Philo: "– yet still judged as double illusion! Metaphysics properly means only objectively mistaken science, never personal interpretation; accordingly, there never really is any personal artistic metaphysics".

Witt: "Philosophers constantly see the method of science before their eyes, and are irresistibly tempted to ask and answer questions in the way that science does. This tendency is the real source of metaphysics, and leads the philosopher into complete darkness. I want to say here that it can never be our job to reduce anything to anything, or to explain anything. Philosophy really *is* 'purely descriptive'" – "our ["philosophical"] considerations could not be scientific ones...And we may not advance any kind of theory. There must not be anything hypothetical in our considerations. We must do away with all *explanation*, and description alone must take its place". I might add: "My fundamental ideas came to me very early in life" – as in 1913 I noted down: "In philosophy there are no deductions: it is purely descriptive".

Philo: "Truly most insightful! It must be said, however, that philosophy is really correctly only some conceptual descriptions and not unsayably 'descriptive' as the *Tractatus* proclaims! And recognizing this, strictly we must stop making fundamental or foundational claims for philosophy and logic about concepts – that are always on the same level, non-hierarchical. Nor is logical truth simply unsayable 'tautology'. For the *Tractatus* holds that the unsayable is only not scientifically sayable as experiential fact".

Witt: What I meant and continue to mean is essentially: "Philosophy is not a theory [nor "doctrine", *Lehre*]". "Grammatical conventions cannot be justified...description already presupposes the grammatical rules".

Philo: "Certainly, any justification or explanation is given in language. Your early logical representational view – or 'picture theory' as might be so called, totally misleadingly, by others – must be no genuine picture or theory at all, and not merely by its own mistaken exclusively scientific standard of only empirical fact having (paradoxically unsayable) sense!"

Nietz: Even after my first book, I wrote of "That impulse towards the formation of metaphors, that fundamental impulse of man" – "our intellect is a mirror...[wherein what] we *call*...cause and effect...we have seen nothing but *pictures*" – through "depersonalization...objective man ...is only...a *mirror*" – and "every great philosophy, which as a whole always says only: this is the picture of all life".

Philo: "Thought is often called reflection; but understanding is not only thinking, or a mirror of representational reflection, even claimed as only poetic, or both logical saying and silent showing. Three very different kinds of understanding are thought, knowledge and conceptual sense".

Nietz: "Science...pounces upon everything knowable...philosophical thinking however is always...on the track of the great and most important discernments".

Witt: "For there seemed to pertain to logic a peculiar depth – a universal significance...[forming] the basis, or essence, of everything empirical". That "can lead us (and did lead me) to think that if anyone utters a sentence and *means* or *understands* it he is operating a calculus according to definite rules". "Frege and Russell made up a calculus which looked to be *the* calculus underlying the correct use of language...but it is not fundamental". "I myself spoke of a 'complete analysis'" – "in the calculus I once described – a calculus to which, misled as I was by a false notion of reduction, I thought that the whole use of propositions must be reducible". "At the root of all this there was a false and idealized picture of the use of language" – "what we call logic plays a different role from that which [I,] Russell and Frege supposed".

Philo: "And if I may add here, Frege, in anticipation of your saying-showing distinction, maintained that: 'A...sign...*expresses* its sense... [and] *designates* its meaning'".

Witt: "Frege appealed to the degree of self-evidence as the criterion of a logical proposition" – "Self-evidence of which Russell has said [illegitimately I thought] so much".

"In the course of our conversations Russell would often exclaim: "Logic's hell!" – And this perfectly expresses the feeling we had when we were thinking about the problems of logic...every time some new linguistic phenomenon occurred to us, it could retrospectively show that our previous explanation [or description] was unworkable. (We felt that language could always make new, and impossible, demands; and that this made all explanation futile.) But that is the difficulty Socrates gets into in trying to give the definition of a concept. Again and again a use of the word emerges that seems not to be compatible with the concept that other uses have led us to form".

Nietz: I have called Socrates "the prototype of *theoretical man*...[who] exemplified...insatiable, optimistic zest for knowledge".

Philo: "Reasoning against all-comers, Socrates actually repeatedly tried to demonstrate, through giving unaccounted for examples, that we do not know what we thought we knew – leaving his antagonists and himself shaking their heads baffled! Then came Plato's dazzling claims to most extraordinary, other worldly, universally necessary Ideas of Pure Reason. And the *Tractatus* follows in the wake of Socrates' vain search for the assumed, demanded, but ever-elusive absolutely complete meanings, which Plato promptly professed to supply – imagined as Ideas!"

Witt: "A characteristic of [so-called] theorists of the past cultural era was wanting to find the a-priori where there wasn't one...to create the 'a priori'".

Nietz: There are "no *a priori* truths" – such claims "are not forms of knowledge at all! They are regulative articles of belief" – "the most general, the emptiest concepts, [are] the last fumes of evaporating reality".

Witt: "What I am opposed to [or "resisting" now] is the concept of some ideal exactitude given us a priori, as it were".

Philo: "We all agree in deed then, for various reasons, that so-called 'Pure' or a priori knowledge, claiming universal necessity deduced in complete principle independent of and prior to all particular experience, is completely mistaken figment of imagination. The a priori is never found or required in actual linguistic practice.

"And now I would be most grateful if the great difference of personal moral interpretation and objective conceptual practice, which is already emphasized between your inspirational works, each drawing upon ancient origins, could begin to be developed more clearly: objectively defined as relatively completely mutually exclusive, and yet never in opposition but complementary".

Circe, Socrates and Plato

Witt: "A definition surely serves to establish the meaning of a sign" – "we take as the criterion of meaning, [either] something which passes in our mind [a "picture" or abstract rule, or]...the use we make of the word or sentence...the picture in our minds is [most usually] connected...with a [same] particular use". "But...a picture...can be variously interpreted".

Philo: "The criterion of meaning is dynamic or static; but any picture can be differently interpreted and that is insufficient for definition".

Witt: "one might explain the word in the same way we do, and have in one's mind the same picture, and one might nevertheless use it in quite a different way. Only that would be highly unnatural to us", that is, for "the way we live".

Nietz: Thus the philosopher too is "guided by Apollo, the interpreter of dreams". "But morality...knows how to 'inspire'...[is] master of...the art of persuasion...morality has shown itself to be the greatest of all mistresses of seduction – and...the actual *Circe of the philosophers*. Why is it that from Plato onwards every philosophical architect in Europe has built in vain?...The correct answer would [be]...that all philosophers were building under the seduction of morality" – "faith in morality".

Philo: "This now marks a shift of emphasis from your claims of amoral art to morality; and admits objective correctness. Even use of the words 'higher' and 'lower' too have a moral or an objective directional sense".

Nietz: There is "a struggle...against the subordination of art to morality. *L'art pour l'art* [Art for art's sake] means: 'the devil take morality!' But this very hostility betrays that moral prejudice is still dominant".

Philo: "But such prejudice, it must be said, applies at the outset here, when in *The Birth of Tragedy* you expressed your instinct turned against morality; and when you proclaimed the tragic evil spell of individuality!"

Nietz: Again, "the Circe of philosophers, morality" – "The Circe of mankind, morality, has falsified".

Philo: "The beautiful sorceress Circe lived on Aeaea, her island of the rising Sun (Helios her father); she was notorious for turning humans into beasts or stone. But even Circe's personal veil cannot objectively falsify.

"This reminds me of another Mediterranean magical island, where Prospero conjured up the tempest for revenge on those who had displaced him. Prospero's magical powers come from the knowledge of his Book; yet he is concerned with more than magic, dream – 'or some enchanted trifle', 'that will not let you believe things certain'. Surely, whoever has written in spellbinding vengeance against life will need to renounce it, vowing 'I'll drown my book' as Prospero did".

Witt: "Philosophy is a battle against the bewitchment of our intelligence by means of language".

Nietz: "We must stride boldly into the thick of those battles...being waged in the highest spheres...between insatiable optimistic knowledge and the tragic need for art...the most *illustrious antagonist* of the tragic view of the world, [being] science".

Philo: "Please be so kind as to elaborate on this Greek Mediterranean birth of dialectics, and its apparent battles, which came to be centred in ancient Athens".

Nietz: "*Tyrants of the spirit* [or "*mind*', *Geist*]...the Greek philosophers ...each...had a firm belief in themselves and in their 'truth'...[even] believing that he possessed 'absolute truth'" – "the war of the opposites... is Hesiod's good Eris [Strife as Striving]...a contest (*agon*)" – that arose too between "such a wonderfully idealised company of philosophers as that of the early Greek masters...All...self-contained...not bound by any convention, because at that time [in the sixth and fifth centuries BC] no professional class of philosophers and scholars existed".

Philo: "In ancient Greece, I understand that being an imposing warlike 'tyrant' was positively envied as most desirable".

Nietz: "the older Greeks felt differently about envy from the way we do. Hesiod counted it among the effects of the good, beneficent Eris". "These philosophers...were tyrants, which is what every Greek wanted to be, and which each one was, if he was *able*".

"I set apart with high reverence the name of *Heraclitus*" – "he denied 'Being' altogether". Affirming: "Everything...is in a state of flux" – "the play of the great world-child, Zeus" – "the eternally living fire" – "all Becoming...the divergence of...opposing actions, striving after reunion. A quality is set continually at variance with itself [its opposite] and separates itself into its opposites". So "desire compels the artist to create ...[who then sits or] stands contemplative above...[having "learned"] antagonism and harmony must pair themselves for the procreation of the work of art". And once more, I held: "Only as an aesthetic phenomenon is the world...eternally justified".

Witt: Also again, while writing my first book, I too believed: "The work of art is the object seen *sub specie aeternitatis* [under the form of eternity]".

Philo: "And I understand that Heraclitus claimed to convey the wise account, *logos*, as the eternal hidden fiery harmony of One ruling over all. It is Zeus' 'thunderbolt' that 'steers all'; 'conflict [or 'strife', *eris*] is justice', by which divine Fate 'all things come to pass', as administered by the Furies. The universe is divided against itself as ceaseless cycle of the 'turnings of fire'; yet Heraclitus saw that Strife also encourages over-coming adversity in a 'harmony' of 'opposites'. Hesiod had distinguished Strife as cruel or healthy competitive striving; but Heraclitus stays silent

20

on this earlier poet explicitly perceiving these two kinds of Eris. And the question now arises: was Heraclitean fire opposed by any kind of watery philosophy?"

Nietz: Parmenides quickly "dived into the cold bath of his awful abstractions. That which is true must exist in eternal presence...indivisible ...immovable...like a globe ["as a resting, dead ball"]...Thus there exists only the eternal Unity...All sense perceptions, Parmenides judges, cause only illusions...Truth is now to dwell only in the most faded, most abstract generalities, in the empty husks of the most indefinite words...now the philosopher sits, bloodless as an abstraction" – "for Parmenides 'Being' and Thinking coincide...since there was not permitted a duality of 'Being'" – "death-like rest of the coldest and emptiest conception, that of the 'Being'...was not striven after as the mystic absorption in *one* all-sufficing enrapturing conception".

Philo: "Such a pale philosopher's too 'pure' rational desire for One eternally fixed, absolutely complete, Necessity admits no spatio-temporal otherness. Parmenides' claim to know One Reality 'Alone, unmoving... being [or 'Being', *einai*]' remains cold metaphysical abstraction".

Witt: "If by eternity is understood not endless temporal duration but timelessness, then he lives eternally who lives in the present". "But is it possible for one so to live that life stops being problematic? That one is living in eternity and not in time?"

Philo: "Since most ancient times, people have felt and believed that suffering the ever-changing world in time is overcome through awareness of a much longer-lasting, even eternal as everlasting or timeless, reality of many deities or One Real Divine Being – sustaining, in and beyond the fleeting and judged illusory world of becoming. Various mystic voices, as heard in India and around the Mediterranean, proclaim "All is One".

"Early Presocratics each assumed a single original, eternal, universal, unifying, impersonal nature or element; for example, 'water' (Thales), 'The Indefinite' (Anaximander), 'mist' (*aêr*, Anaximenes), 'number' (duality of Limit and Unlimited; Pythagoras) or – it must be added – 'fire' (Heraclitus). But any such absolute view of the whole, *oulos*, or universe, *kosmos*, monistically reduced to so-called knowledge that 'All is One', or 'The Many originates from the One', remains a senseless claim of the mystical metaphysician. Thus one might say that Circe, bewitching immorality, transformed these earliest Western 'natural' philosophers into tyrants of the spirit".

Nietz: "The One, [means] flight from the Becoming".

Then came "Socrates...and what indeed did he do all his life long but ["reason" and] laugh at the clumsy incapacity of his noble Athenians, who...were never able to supply adequate information about the reasons for their actions. Ultimately, however, in silence and secrecy, he [surely] laughed at himself too: he found...the same difficulty...[He concluded:]

21

one must follow the instincts, but [also] persuade reason to aid [or "support"] them with good arguments. This was the actual *falsity* of [Socrates]...he had seen through [to, or "perceived"] the irrational aspect of the moral judgment".

Philo: "As said a little earlier, Socrates repeatedly left one and all baffled. But to make the claim that there never is any genuine knowledge is indeed actual falsity, as some conceptual kind of particular knowledge – that is a rational objective certainty!"

Witt: "Reading the Socratic dialogues one has the feeling: what a frightful waste of time! What's the point of these arguments that prove nothing and clarify nothing?" – "Socrates keeps reducing the sophist to silence...the sophist does not know what he thinks he knows; but that is no triumph for Socrates. It can't [even] be a case of...'So none of us knows anything!'" Again: "A definition surely serves to establish the meaning of a sign". "I need a criterion of identity".

Nietz: We are "led by instinctive moral definitions". There is "no *criterion of truth*, but an *imperative* [of morality] concerning that which *should* count as true".

Witt: At long last after the *Tractatus*, I began explicitly to recognize relative sense in practice, with the following distinction. "I call 'symptom' a phenomenon of which experience has taught us that it coincided, in some way or other, with...our defining criterion...[Although some words have "clearly defined meanings"] in general we don't use language according to strict rules...[like] a calculus proceeding according to exact rules...We are unable clearly to circumscribe the concepts we use... because there is no real [one] 'definition' to them...[By] Socrates' question "What is knowledge?"...an exact definition...is ["mistakenly"] asked for. As the problem is put, it seems that there is something wrong with the ordinary use of the word 'knowledge'. It appears we don't know what it means, and that therefore, perhaps, we have no right to use it. We should reply: "There is no one exact usage of the word 'knowledge'"...Many words...don't have a strict meaning. But this is not a defect. To think it is would be like saying that the light of my reading lamp is no real light at all because it has no sharp boundary...A word has the meaning someone has given to it...we [philosophers wrongly] thought we could improve on ordinary language. But ordinary language is all right. Whenever we make up 'ideal languages' it is not in order to replace our ordinary language... our method is not merely to enumerate actual usages of words, but rather deliberately to invent [to "compare"] new ones, some of them because of their absurd appearance".

Philo: "Very perceptively and clearly said – and not sharply defined! For many concepts, there is no one and only exact, *the* correct, use".

Witt: Again, "sense" is not "sharply bounded" – "'sense' is vague" – itself "a concept with blurred edges".

Philo: "Conceptual sense expresses dynamic, incomplete essence of everyday realizable meaning; sense is relatively both arbitrary, vague, and not arbitrary, essential. Philosophy makes only sufficiently clear different objective kinds of either senses or senselessness in practice".

Witt: "Socrates fails to produce a definition of 'knowledge' because there is no definition giving what is common to all instances of knowledge. Because the word 'knowledge' is used in all sorts of ways, any definition given will fail to apply to some cases...The [Socratic] method of giving a definition of a word and then proceeding to other instances of its application which have very little in common is a mistaken method". "I cannot give a full grammatical description...of the use of words...all we in fact do is give a few examples and explanations [or descriptions]...no more than this is necessary".

Philo: "I should add here, that ancient Greek mathematicians, over a thousand years after the Babylonians, came to realize some geometrical magnitudes cannot be expressed as a ratio of whole numbers; although it is disputed exactly who in the fifth century BC recognized the 'irrational' (*alogos*). Hippasus departed from the strict Pythagorean ways of perfect spheres and not publishing discoveries. A story is told too of the drowning of the mathematical revealer of irrationality; yet it is said as well that the Pythagoreans, due to their code of not causing harm, only symbolically killed the 'traitor' – who had publicized the 'irrationality' of numbers – by inscribing his name on a tomb. So the drowning may express a soul adrift with no standard of measurement [see References]. And in terms of the Pythagorean divine 'marriage', the clear and whole numerical rationality of Apollo cannot contain or harmonize the 'irrational' excesses of Eris.

"An irrational number, so called in modern terms, cannot be expressed exactly as a fraction, a ratio of two whole numbers. Thus not everything is commensurate as whole number proportion; any such measurement must be incomplete. There never is any absolutely universal distinct *atomon* ('uncuttable' or 'indivisible') whole unit of measure. Hence, irrational numbers are only really 'irrational' from a naively limited perspective of whole number rationality. They demonstrate the impossibility of any a priori atom of measurement. And this supplies a clue – which most unfortunately Socrates, Plato, Aristotle and others were to ignore – that incommensurability applies to ordinary concepts. There cannot be any reduction of everyday language in terms of either conceptual or 'logical' atomism. Completely clear and sharp universal so-called conceptual definition is only an unrealizable ideal of the metaphysician".

Nietz: Initially I wrote of "those old sages from Thales to Socrates" – in later contrast to whom "the philosophers are the *décadents* of Hellenism, the counter-movement against the old, noble taste...The Socratic virtues were preached *because* the Greeks had lost them". But questions arose about "that which brought about the death of tragedy:

the Socratism of morality, the dialectics...could not that very Socratism be a symptom of decline...?" – "Might the scientific approach be... morally speaking, something like cowardice and [objectively] falsehood? Amorally speaking, a piece of [vengeful] cunning?" And finally Socrates, "at the last moment of his life...he said: "O Crito, I owe Asclepius a rooster". This ridiculous and terrible 'last word' means for those who have ears: "O Crito, life is a disease"...[He apparently] had lived cheerfully... while concealing...Socrates *suffered life!*"

Philo: "This conviction for the need of such violent blood-sacrifice, to the physician Asclepius, reveals Socrates maintained a hateful curse on life as sickness, for which – to heal the soul – the only cure is death".

Nietz: "Was Socrates after all a corrupter of youths, and deserved his hemlock?"

Philo: "– never actually according to at least the Pythagoreans!"

Nietz: "The appearance of the Greek philosophers from Socrates onwards is a symptom of decadence; the...decline of Greece". Once more, I first believed that: "Those moralists...who, following in the footsteps of Socrates, offer the individual a morality of self-control and temperance as a means to his own advantage, as his personal key to happiness, are the exceptions...they cut themselves off from the community". But "Socrates [and thereby "the mob"]...achieved by means of it ["dialectics"] victory over a more noble taste...Besides, one [as ruler] mistrusted such public presentation of one's arguments [or "reasons"]...There is something indecent about showing all one's cards [or "goods"]. What can be "demonstrated" [or "has to be proved"] is of little worth". Thus "the dialectical hero of the Platonic drama", "Socrates for the first time recognized as an agent of Hellenic disintegration, as a typical décadent. 'Rationality' *against* instinct...undermining life".

Philo: "So ancient Greek tragedy, blazing as a meteor, was short-lived. And, undoubtedly, Socrates was Plato's greatest philosophical inspiration. Out of reverence, Plato takes the great liberty of placing his own vision of Forms into the mouth of the figure he portrays as Socrates. Plato followed Socrates in assuming purely intelligible Knowledge of universal essences and the utter inadequacy of relative knowledge; but in the last dialectical analysis Socrates denied whereas Plato affirmed the necessary existence of perfect Knowledge of Ideas. Socrates' vainly searched for the assumed, but entirely unrealistically demanded, ever-elusive absolutely complete meanings, which Plato promptly professed to supply imagined as Ideas!"

Nietz: "I know of nothing more venomous than the joke Epicurus... [made] against Plato and the Platonists; he called them *Dionysiokolakes* ...[deceitful] 'flatterers of Dionysus'...*actors*, there is nothing genuine about them". Thus "did Plato flee from reality and desire to see things only in pallid mental pictures". "Plato is a coward in face of reality – consequently he flees into the ideal".

Philo: "Following with all speed after Parmenides and Socrates, Plato created the first developed representational philosophy in Europe. And if I may now make this a little clearer: Plato's kind of double vision claims that known worldly objects are only imitations, copies of non-sensory, purely intelligible Knowledge – that is 'the science of dialectic' of eternal, perfect, Real Forms, absolutely complete ideals. Plato's Socrates claims earthly knowledge is always imperfect, partial recollection (*anamnesis*) of Forms; the immortal soul Knows all these Essences before its rebirths.

"Further, Plato claimed Forms of all worldly objects, excepting artistic creations. He saw the theatre as vulgar, bad taste, profane, dishonourable imitation, at best concealing genuine reality. All poetry is condemned as poisonous without 'the antidote in a knowledge of its real nature', and the imitative artist 'understands only the appearance, and not the reality'. For Plato (in the voice of his Socrates) all dramatic compositions of the poets are 'phantoms' of imitation, 'twice removed' from real knowledge, that is, copies of representations of Forms. Plato denounced drama as doubly deceptive imitation of illusion, to be banished from the ideal society, except for serious praises to the gods or virtue.

"Lastly about this, I should mention again that any sharp opposition between Apollo and Dionysus is too clear-cut, that is, to some extent too Apolline; as, contra the impression often given in *The Birth of Tragedy*, music is not exclusively Dionysian. And Plato even restricts the kind of music allowed in the ideal state: admitting as more refined Apollo's stringed instruments, the lyre and lute, while banning the shrill pipes of the satyr Marsyas". [For all these Plato quotes see References.]

Nietz: "What did the Greeks admire in Odysseus? Above all, his capacity for lying [objective deception], and for cunning...having all means at his command...all this is the Greek ideal!"

Philo: "But still, Plato's view of 'pure' intelligibility disapproves vehemently of 'tragedy and its leader, Homer'; and even claims 'there is a quarrel of long standing between philosophy and poetry...an old antagonism' – extending from Plato and Socrates back to Homer, about 150 years before the very first Greek 'natural' philosophers. And I see in *The Birth of Tragedy*, expressing in a different way art as 'the illusion of illusion', you too strode boldly into the thick of this so-called battle".

Nietz: "Plato versus Homer: that is the complete, the real antagonism – on the one side, the sincerest 'man of the beyond', the philosopher who most defames life; on the other, the poet who involuntarily [glorifies and] deifies it, the *golden* nature".

"Plato...honoured and deified the concept as an ideal Form" – "in the entire history of philosophy there *is* no intellectual integrity – but only [so-called] 'love of the good'" – "the most dangerous of [objective] errors hitherto ["in Europe"] has been...Plato's invention of Pure Spirit and the Good in Itself" – as "eternal treasure".

Philo: "The Homeric tradition, in glorifying war, falsifies the terrible realities of barbaric destruction, pain and enslavement.

"And any claimed quarrel between the poet, expressing personal sentiment, and either the scientist or the philosopher emphasizing respectively particular known or essential kind of objectivity, is actually mistaken. Reason and poetry are never genuinely opponents, for they cannot contradict each other.

"Plato's view misjudges art as merely the sleeper's dream; his vision expresses disenchantment of art taken as not art but imitation; and *The Birth of Tragedy*, it must be said, uncritically follows this overlooking of art as such. Again, to criticize a work of art for being only representative of apparent reality, even as compared to Absolute Reality, fails to admit genuine kinds of reality, including art as personal reality".

Witt: "there is nothing which explains [or describes] the meanings of words as well as a picture". But in the *Tractatus*, "to call a proposition a "picture" was misleading". "A *picture* held us captive".

Philo: "– due to seemingly scientific desire for a priori logical form of picturing, going back in the West to Plato. If the first Mediterranean highly influential philosophy developed of representationalism – and indeed the rational Pure Good – had not come from Plato, it would have come soon enough from another metaphysician!

"Eventually, it was Kant who attempted to unite empirical and rational philosophical traditions, based upon assuming things-in-themselves, noumena, admitted as unknowable yet still described as the needed real substantial cause of representational veiling. As metaphysician Kant claimed that all possible knowledge must be representational phenomena conforming to a priori concepts of universally necessary objectivity. Kant's influential so-called critical system is actually uncritical, mistaken, incurably representational, unrealizable idealistic imagination! Kantian Noumenon, essence behind apparent phenomena, is then identified by Schopenhauer through Platonic Ideas and Indian mysticism as Will – next called Dionysian Will – Kant's unknowable thing-in-itself is replaced by known will in itself. Kantian metaphysics is not rejected only deepened!"

Nietz: "Oh how [objectively] false is...such...a critique of reason as a whole...that the intellect itself should 'know'...its own limitations? was it not even a little absurd?" – "it is [objectively] not true that the essence of things [in themselves] appears [represented] in the empiric world".

As I have already said concerning *The Birth of Tragedy*, "How I now regret that I did not...permit myself *a new language*...to express strange and new evaluations".

Philo: "I understand that you next began to write of artistic illusion of illusion – not in mystical Dionysian and Apolline terms but – in a new higher moral or ultramoral (*aussermoralischen*) sense, beyond good and evil of traditional morality. Please could you now elaborate on this".

Nietz: Some two years after finishing my first book, I still held that "the expression of every deep philosophical intuition by means of dialectics and scientific reflection is...the only means to communicate ...but...metaphorical". More specifically, I wrote: "If he [man] does not mean to content himself with tautology, that is, with empty husks, he will always obtain illusions instead of truth. What is a word? The expression of a nerve-stimulus in sounds. But to infer a cause outside us is already [objectively] a wrong and unjustifiable application...[That is so-called] truth with the genesis of language...how indeed should we dare to say: the stone is hard; as if "hard" was...not merely an entirely subjective stimulus! ...A nerve-stimulus, first transformed into a percept [or "image"; an object produced]...again copied into [or "imitated by"] a sound!...[In] language ...we only possess metaphors...; truths are illusions of which one has forgotten that they *are* illusions...and by *this very unconsciousness*...as a "*rational*" being he [man] submits his actions to the sway of abstractions; he no longer suffers himself to be carried away by sudden impressions, by sensations, he first generalizes all these impressions into paler cooler ideas [or "less colourful concepts"]...resolving a perception ["first impressions"] into an idea [or "to dissolve an image into a concept"]... [Thus] the illusion of the artistic metamorphosis...truth...is of very limited value, I mean it is anthropomorphic through and through...understanding of the world as a human-like thing...man as the measure of all things...: in short only...as an *artistically creating* subject...does he live with[in]... the prison walls of this faith".

Witt: "What is the meaning of a word? Let us attack this question". Again, "a picture...can be variously interpreted...stands isolated...dead" – "sense...the life of the sign, we should have to say...[is] its *use*". "Language is an instrument. Its concepts are instruments". Hence "the multiplicity of the tools in language and of the ways they are used".

Philo: "Yes, concepts are certainly tools, that is, more of less practical techniques, of different objective kinds of descriptions".

Nietz: At that time I further wrote: "the insect and the bird perceive a world different from his [man's] own, and the question, which of the two [or three] world-perceptions is more accurate, is quite [objectively] a senseless one, since to decide this question it would be necessary to apply the standard of *right perception* which *does not exist* – for between two utterly different spheres, as between subject and object, there is no causality, no *accuracy*, but at the utmost an *aesthetical* stammering translation, that artistic formation of metaphors, with which every sensation in us begins, the formation of metaphors, that fundamental impulse of man".

Witt: "There cannot be a question whether these or other [earlier: "grammatical"] rules are the correct ones...For without these rules the word [so called] has as yet no meaning".

That aside: "There really are cases where someone has the sense of what he wants to say much more clearly in his mind than he can express in words. (This happens to me very often.)". "I never more than half succeed in expressing what I want to express. Actually not as much as that, but by no more than a tenth. That is still worth something. Often my writing is nothing but 'stuttering'".

Nietz: "every creature different from us...lives in a different world from that in which we live...to demand that our human interpretations and values should be universal...is...madness of human pride".

Witt: But "only of a living human being and what resembles (behaves like) a living human being can one say: it has sensations...is conscious or unconscious".

Philo: "The world is certainly other than primarily centring in mankind – plainly not everything relatively in itself is human or anthropocentric. But how could one live only as a stuttering poet, creating all the world as only illusory artistic double metaphorical metamorphosis? How could our rationality be so unconsciously creative, dominant in and of the world?

"Human nature is an essential part of Nature as rationally so called. Again Nature as itself objective defined fact is always amoral, unaesthetic and unreligious. But different species interact, and differences to human nature are always conceptually so recognized; our rational consciousness pervades, relates, all people, bodies, perceptions and things. For example, a stone is not rational or living, but only recognized as such through the rational word 'stone'. The inescapable given context relating any meaning, rationally so called, must be at least human conceptual and behavioural everyday practice. Definitions, as both sense and reference, relate all meanings; the terms of any metaphorical, or any other rational expression, must be objectively defined. Accordingly, not all language can be poetry.

(facing Nietzsche) "Your artist's so-called metaphysics mistreats anthropomorphism 'through and through' as if universally necessary Measure, just like the a priori. Human language is relatively universal, not Absolutely Universal. The world is always relatively not Absolutely so called in human terms; other than human language, meaning or culture is only to some extent like or unlike human language, meaning or culture".

Nietz: A "tyrant...[of] conditions...imposed as a law...fails to perceive ...its relativity". "Words are only symbols for the relations of things" – "past and future are as unreal as any dream...everything...in space and time, has only a relative existence" – "everything has evolved [or "become"]...nor are there any absolute Truths".

Philo (now turning to Wittgenstein): "And if I may bring you in here, concerning this essential relativity of linguistic meaning, on your return, still maintaining the claim of the *Tractatus* that ethics is unsayable, you proceeded to give 'A Lecture on Ethics', expressing perception of seeming yet senseless absolutely complete Value".

Witt: I said, "our words will only express facts; as a teacup will only hold a teacup full of water and [even] if I were to pour a gallon over it... there is only relative value...I wonder...'how extraordinary that anything should exist'...But it is nonsense to say that I wonder at the existence of the world ["whatever it is"] because I cannot imagine it not existing".

Philo: "– as the *Tractatus* claims that any genuine truth, or falsity, must be deniable, scientific empirical fact".

Witt: I further said, unscientific "misuse of our language runs through all ethical and religious expressions...the absolute miraculous remains nonsense...I [too] wanted...to go beyond the [factual] world...beyond significant [scientific] language...all...who ever tried to write or talk Ethics or Religion...run against the boundaries of language...the walls of our cage [that] is perfectly, absolutely hopeless. But...I personally cannot help respecting [it] deeply and I would not for my life ridicule it".

"humans will continue to bump [or "run"] up against the same mysterious difficulties, and stare...longing for the supra-natural, for in believing that they see the 'limits of human understanding' of course they believe that they can see beyond it".

Philo: "For, surely, a limit is conceivable only from both sides"

Witt: Again: "Aesthetically, the miracle is that the world exists". But I still confusingly held: "the astonishment that anything exists...Everything which we feel like [or try] saying [of such paradox] can, a priori, only be nonsense...misunderstanding...Yet...points to [or "indicates"] something". But, to repeat, I came to recognize that: "No sign leads us beyond itself". "If you understand at all you understand a proposition...in a system".

Philo: "What then of the elucidatory ladder of philosophy having to be used then discarded, and the self-ridiculingly so called ever unsayable?"

Witt: "Anything that I might reach by climbing a ladder does not interest me" – "a nothing would serve just as well as a something about which nothing could be said".

Philo (turning to Nietzsche): "And how, may I now ask, did you next develop upon the artistic illusion of illusion in a higher moral sense?"

Nietz: Some six years on, I wrote: "*In prison*...I live...I cannot escape. Around every being there is described a similar concentric circle... peculiar to him...a comparable circle...within which each of us encloses his senses as if behind prison walls...we measure the world...and it is all of it an error (*Irrthümer*)!...our senses have woven us into lies and deception (*Lug und Trug*) of sensation: these again are the basis of all our judgments and 'knowledge' – there is absolutely no escape, no backway or bypath into the *real world* [in itself]!" – only "a brazen wall of fate: we *are* in prison, we can only *dream* ourselves free, not make ourselves free".

Philo: "Is that not your early view, following Schopenhauer on a dark pessimistic path? For he too claimed, 'we therefore come up against...the walls of our prison...of...representation'" [for fuller quote see References].

Nietz: I accordingly went on: "we catch nothing at all except that which allows itself to be caught in precisely *our* net...We understand nothing of him ["our neighbour"] except the *change in us* of which he is the [believed] cause...We attribute to him the sensations his actions evoke in us, and thus bestow upon him a false, inverted positivity. According to our knowledge of ourself we make of him a satellite of our own system ...we are the ultimate cause...we nonetheless believe the opposite! World of phantoms in which we live! Inverted, upside-down, empty world, yet dreamed of as *full* and *upright*!"

Philo: "I see in this 'interpretation' that you make claims not only to objective error, but also to each of us as absolutely completely Alone – which would be intolerably self-orientated, far too self-isolating.

"I also hear an echo of Schopenhauer describing: 'Life...as a fleeting ...light morning dream...which [does]...deceive; and...finally vanish' [for fuller quote see References]. And what's more, an echo of Wagner's wonderful highly romantic opera *Tristan and Isolde* (of 1859), with its tragic *libretto* permeated however by the dark mood of Schopenhauer's philosophy. As, for instance, Tristan sings: 'Day's phantoms! Morning dreams, deceiving and desolate! Vanish! Away!'; and finally Isolde, with her dying words 'unconscious, supreme joy!' (*unbewusst, höchste Lust!*), as if transfigured, sinks upon Tristan's lifeless body. At last released from suffering the seeming emptiness of life, the two lovers are wholly united, free from all dreams in deepest sleep, complete unconsciousness!"

Nietz: Citing "the two most famous and pronounced romantics whom I *misunderstood*...This...*romantic pessimism* ["dissatisfaction with reality"] ...[of] Schopenhauer's philosophy of will or Wagner's music" – expresses "weariness with life" – "that nerve-destroying music [I heard from 1868] and metaphysical philosophy [I read first from 1865]" – "Schopenhauer's scandalous misunderstanding...took art for...denial of life". "One summer at Bayreuth [in 1876] I became fully conscious of all this". "I saw the great...seduction...the will turning *against* life". I saw "tragedy...of the sufferings of *others*...also...making oneself suffer...[man's] dangerous thrills of cruelty directed *against himself*".

"Schopenhauer's metaphysics...is false" – "metaphysical befogging of everything" – "my great teacher Schopenhauer": "he misunderstood genius, art itself, morality, pagan religion, beauty, knowledge, and more or less everything" – "he blundered in everything". "Schopenhauer spoke of 'will'; but nothing is more characteristic of his philosophy than the absence of all genuine willing". "Schopenhauer was hostile to life".

Philo: "I understand that Wagner 'first came across' Schopenhauer's *Die Welt als Wille und Vorstellung* in the autumn of 1854, and within a year read it four times; later recording that book 'certainly exerted a decisive influence on the whole course of my life'. During that year of 1855, Wagner mentions being 'under the influence of Schopenhauer and a profound realization of the intense tragedy of life and the emptiness of its phenomena' – 'the serious mood created by Schopenhauer, which was trying to find ecstatic expression. It was some such mood that inspired the conception of a Tristan and Isolde'". [For further details see References.]

Nietz: "*Tristan*: it is a masterpiece and casts a spell which is unmatched not only in music but in all the arts". Nonetheless, after receiving [on 3.1. 1878] a copy of Wagner's *Parsifal* 'poem' [the complete libretto], "I went on alone...weary of the whole idealistic pack of [artistic] lies...all romantic music...[is] oppressive art that deprives the spirit of its very severity and cheerfulness and lets rampant every kind of vague longing" – "the [stage-] actor should not become the corrupter of the genuine...music should not become an art of lying" – "not just mistaken, but *lying*. That's after all what 'beautiful souls' do who can't bear to look reality in the face".

Philo: "Now you clearly objectively judged art as not just double untruth, illusion of illusion, nor just mistaken but cowardly lie".

Nietz: '*in the "Birth of Tragedy"*...one encounters...gloomy and unpleasant...pessimism...[judging the] *one* world...is false, cruel...without meaning...*We have need of lies* (*Lüge*)...to live...man must be a liar...above all an *artist*. And he *is* one: metaphysics, religion, morality, science – all of them only products of his will to art, to lie, to flight from 'truth'...Art... is the great means of making life possible...the great stimulant of life. Art as the only superior counterforce to...nihilism...The will to appearance, to illusion...to objectified deception...[in relation to this] the author... knows...that art is *worth more* than truth". For "nihilism...[is] the belief in absolute *worthlessness*, i.e., *meaning*lessness". "A nihilist...judges... the world...ought *not* to be, and...as it ought to be...does not exist...our existence (action, suffering, willing, feeling) has no meaning".

Philo: "To call art the only 'superior' power and 'worth more than truth', expresses not purely artistic but also moral judgment. And 'objectified deception', through which one 'knows' the value of art, would be not just disenchanted but senseless, unutterable, if objectivity itself were illusory. The word 'lie', 'error', 'mistake' or 'correct' is validly used, makes sense, really to mean an objective judgment, whether explicitly admitted or not.

"The nihilist too creates meaning as moral judgment, including self-defeating meaninglessness of that very belief. But one should recognize that if the world is cruel then it is morally so judged, and if illusory then objectively so; or if meaningless then neither moral nor immoral and neither true nor false. Statements about Nature as particular objectivity are factual truth or falsity and neither moral nor immoral.

"Even your interlocutor in *The Birth of Tragedy* saw 'hatred [of life] ...in your ['pessimistic...befogging'] artist's metaphysics...the familiar romantic...collapse before an old faith'. So many metaphysicians and artists, including romantics, as ascetics turned against life, have painted a seductively tragic and dark picture of life as empty, even evil; yearning for a religious or artistic Realm of Light absolutely beyond – as conscious or even unconscious highest bliss!"

Nietz: "Richard Wagner...a despairing romantic" – to his art of music-drama I dedicated *The Birth of Tragedy* – yet "one should not let oneself be misled about him by his own misunderstandings". Nevertheless, "I am still grateful to him for having inspired me to strive passionately for independence of spirit".

Philo: "And to some extreme contrasting extent, the so-called will-less and selfless ascetic expresses contempt for, despises, individual embodied life; proclaiming all the world as merely apparent fleeting illusion".

Nietz: "In individual moments we all know...we realize...and are amazed at...the whole dreamlike condition in which we live...we...raise our head above the water...even if only a little, and observe what stream it is in which we are so deeply immersed".

Witt: I too once wrote, "Our life is like a dream. But in our better hours we wake up just enough to realize that we are dreaming. Most of the time, though, we are fast asleep".

Nietz: "If we had not welcomed the arts and invented this kind of cult of the untrue (*Unwahren*), then...the realization that delusion and error are conditions of human knowledge and sensation – [that] would be utterly unbearable. *Honesty* would lead to nausea and suicide. But now there is ...art as the good [moral "conscience" and] will to appearance".

Witt: But "it's strange that those who ascribe reality only to things [in themselves; or to poetry, another world or One Reality] and not to our ideas [or behaviour]...move so unquestioningly in the world...This which we take as a matter of course [given], life, is supposed to be something accidental, subordinate [or "unimportant"]; while something that normally never comes into my head, reality!"

Philo: "Also, to speak of the application of rules or sense may mislead; not least pointing to something and saying 'This is called X'".

Witt: "The ostensive definition of signs is not an *application* of language, but part of the grammar" – "there is no [such] confrontation of a sign [or "language"] with reality. In the *Tractatus* logical analysis and ostensive definition were unclear to me". One clue was: "Such words [and logical connectives] as 'and', 'not', 'or', etc. obviously do not stand for anything". Early on I noted: "The meaning of a proposition is a fact which actually corresponds to it"; but really "in no case is a word 'representative' of its meaning, although a proper name is 'representative' of its bearer".

Philo: "In other words, a name represents its specific known contingent reference, never its essential sense. There is no such defining connection between language and reality – already so called – such representational view, which has dominated the history of philosophy, is only a fiction!"

Witt: "Grammar is not accountable to any reality. It is grammatical rules that determine meaning (constitute it) and so they themselves are not answerable to any meaning and to that extent are arbitrary" – "grammar ...what makes it not arbitrary is its use". "What we call [conceptual] "*descriptions*" are instruments for particular uses".

Nietz: "as if there were an actual *drive for* [particular] *knowledge* that, without regard to questions of ["separate from...[moral] *practical* interests"] usefulness and harm, went blindly for the truth".

Witt: "given a set of axioms [or premises or pictures] and rules, we could imagine different ways of using them...What is necessary is determined by the rules...We must distinguish between a necessity in the system and a necessity of the system as a whole".

Philo: "Once more, we must distinguish two entirely different kinds of senses of judged necessary rules for following a practice: as moral neither correct nor error, or as objective in a system".

Nietz: "How is truth proved?...by utility – by indispensability – in short, by advantages (namely, presuppositions concerning what truth *ought* to be like for us to recognize it). But that is a [moral] prejudice" – "only certain truths are admitted".

Witt: "Is it wrong for me to be guided in my actions by the propositions of physics?...Isn't precisely this what we call a 'good ground'? Supposing we met people who did not regard this as a telling reason...Instead of the physicist, they consult an oracle [as at Delphi]...Is it wrong...?...At the end of [giving] reasons comes *persuasion*".

"it has no meaning to say that a game [or objective practice] has always been played wrong". "Whether a thing is a blunder or not – it is a blunder in a particular system" – "rules can't collide, unless they contradict each other...without these ["grammatical"] rules the word has as yet no meaning; and if we change the rules, it now has another meaning (or none), and in that case we may just as well change the word too...if you follow other rules than those of chess, you are playing another game; and if you follow grammatical rules other than such-and-such ones, that does not mean you say something wrong, no, you are speaking of something else". "If I change the rules it is a different game".

Philo: "Changing an alphabet, or a set of sign characters, changes that language partially or completely. Again, the words 'necessity', 'right' and 'wrong' have subjective or objective kinds of senses. Accordingly, such contrasting kinds of practical guidance, which you just mentioned, are never opposing, never as such correct or mistaken, but totally different".

Witt: Further: "If I say: here we are at the limits of language, then it always sounds as if resignation were necessary; whereas on the contrary, complete satisfaction comes, since no question remains" – "philosophy does not call on me for any sacrifice ["of understanding"], because I am not denying myself the saying of anything but simply giving up a certain combination of words as senseless". "Time and again the attempt is made to use language to limit the world and set it in relief – but it can't be done".

Nietz: "Language depends on the most naïve prejudices...we think *only* in the form of language [earlier: "grey concepts"]...we barely reach the doubt that sees this limitation as a limitation. Rational thought is interpretation according to a scheme that we cannot throw off".

Witt: And "'aren't you neglecting something [I also hear you say]...*the world* behind the mere words?...that which goes without saying...life...as consciousness...the very essence of experience'...But what more can I do ...Isn't what you reproach me of as though you said: 'In your language you're only *speaking*!'"

"When I talk about language (words, sentences, etc.) I must speak the [later: our familiar "full-blown"] language of every day. Is this language somehow too coarse and material for what we want to say?...questions [for example]...had to be expressed in this language, if there was anything to ask!" – "We are only interested in what can be symbolized".

Philo (turning to Nietzsche): "In addition, how could we ever reach and recognize the limitations of such claimed universal perception in any objectively distinguished kind of sense – even an ultramoral or higher than traditional moral sense? And once more, you now refer gloomily to 'the philosophy of grey concepts...that we cannot throw off', rather than dancing joyfully with colourful essential conceptual meanings!"

Nietz: "Truth is ugly. We possess *art* lest we *perish of the truth*".

Philo: "– that all, except this sole truth, is lie! How ugly that aesthetic statement would be if true! Worry not in this way: for the poet can never tell a lie! The artist as essentially subjective is free to dream or interpret, but never objective. Again, correctness or mistake recognizes objectivity as genuine; and to condemn art as unreal or lie is a real blunder. Indeed, what first you wrote of pale Parmenides applies here: 'All that plurality, diversity and variety of the empirically known world...is thrown aside mercilessly as mere appearance and delusion...eternal fraud of the senses'".

Witt: To give yet another example: "The solipsist flutters and flutters in the flyglass, strikes against the walls, flutters further". And the "aim in philosophy? – To shew the fly the way out of the fly-bottle", that is to say, of misleading "thoughts".

Philo: "– of the so-called philosophical cage, prison, black box or fly-bottle of deceiving difficulties, false statements made about life!"

Witt: "Running against the limits of language? Language is, after all, not a cage".

Philo: "– that again is contra the long and widespread dark 'selfless' ascetic tradition, as uncritically followed by, for instance, Schopenhauer: proclaiming a pessimistic and mistaken representational view of all life as 'prison', from which attempted escape is entirely hopeless. Freedom from mistaken idealism surely realizes individual wilful actions that cease to be so harmfully turned against oneself and life. And this (facing Nietzsche) to a very significant extent anticipates the rise of your 'free thinking'".

Revaluation of Moral Ideals

Nietz: "We should not let ourselves be tyrannized over by our fairest ability – that of elevating things into the ideal".

With "my 'free thinking'", since [HH] 1876, at last "I liberated myself from...ideal things, [in which] *I* see – human, alas all too human things!" – "human, all too human folly". With "the daybreak of spiritual freedom", this dawning conscious of the falsity of traditional idealism, the "lust for power of idealists of every description", I began to realize freedom from "the will turning *against* life".

"*Twilight of the Idols (Götzen-Dämmerung), or: How to Philosophize with a Hammer*" – "in plain terms: the old truth is coming to an end". "To overthrow idols (my word for 'ideals')...is my business". "I am herewith the *destroyer par excellence*".

Witt: Likewise, "I was thinking about my philosophical work and saying to myself: 'I destroy, I destroy, I destroy'".

Nietz: I also wrote that "the good artist's or thinker's imagination is continually producing things good, mediocre, and bad, but his *power of judgment*, highly sharpened and practised, rejects, selects...All great men were great workers, untiring not only in invention but also in rejecting, sifting, reforming, arranging".

Witt: I read that passage, which in other words asserts "even the best poets and thinkers have written stuff that is mediocre and bad, but have separated off the good material. But it is not quite like that...Something that looks like a bad sentence can be the *germ* of a good one".

Philo: "Even so, the good material is what is harvested".

Witt: "Where does our investigation get its importance from, since it seems only to destroy everything interesting, that is, all that is great and important? (As it were all the buildings, leaving behind only bits of stone and rubble.) What we are destroying is nothing but houses of cards and we are clearing up the ground of language on which they stand".

Nietz: A philosophical "building can be destroyed and *nonetheless* possess value as material", that is, its "bricks...used...for better building".

Witt: "All that philosophy can do is to destroy idols. And that means not creating a new one".

Philo: "The philosopher needs to break the spell of objectively false ideals, which are insubstantial, unrealizable linguistic misunderstandings, yet also needs to help create new genuine ideals of individuality".

Nietz: "when man gets beyond superstitious and religious concepts [of the herd]...at this ["very high"] level of liberation [one] must still... overcome metaphysics...[The] most enlightened...free themselves of metaphysics" – "the end of metaphysical views" that, to repeat, means "the old [so-called] truth is coming to an end".

Philo: "– for just a few, more independent, individuals".

Witt: "Religious faith and superstition are quite [or "entirely", *ganz*] different. One of them results [or "springs", *entspringt*] from fear and is a sort of false science. The other is a [personal] trusting".

I may add that, at the outbreak of war in 1914, when posted to Krakow, I bought volume eight of your collected *Works* (including *Twilight of the Idols* and *The Anti-Christ*), Nietzsche. I was "very troubled" by your "hostility to Christianity". But I had also found Tolstoy's *Gospel in Brief*: "At this time, this book virtually kept me alive".

Philo: "Shocked, shaken, yet still not stirred by the Anti-Christ? May I suggest, however, that later we turn our attention to religious language expressing personal beliefs". This was met by a brief silence of consent.

Nietz: "the highest mountains...arise from the sea...The highest must arise to its height from the deepest".

Philo: "People often claim absolutely complete Highest Ideals, but any realizable ideal of freedom is surely relatively above bondage below".

Witt: "We have got on to slippery ice where there is no friction and so in a certain sense the conditions are ideal, but also, just because of that, we are unable to walk. We want to walk: so we need *friction*. Back to the rough ground!"

Nietz: Sustained "longer duration of elevated feelings...[means] a continual ascent...and...resting on clouds" – "the misty valley below".

In some such situation [see References] I wrote the poem 'Sils Maria':

> "Here sat I, waiting, waiting, – yet not for anything,
> Beyond good and evil, now the light
> Drinking in, now the shadows, all but play,
> All lake, all midday, all time without aim.
> Then, suddenly, friend! one became as two
> – and Zarathustra passed by near to me...".

Witt: "I summed up my [earlier] attitude to philosophy when I said: philosophy ought really to be written only as a poetic composition (*Philosophie dürfte man eigentlich nur dichten*)" – but I had already recognized that "*unpoetic* mentality, which heads straight for what is concrete...is characteristic of my philosophy". "There are problems I never get anywhere near, which do not lie in my path or are not part of my world. Problems of the intellectual world of the West that Beethoven [later: "epic poets"]...tackled and wrestled with, but which no philosopher has ever confronted (perhaps Nietzsche [you] passed by them)...In this world (mine) there is no tragedy...It is as though everything were soluble in the [imagined a priori] aether of the world, there are no hard surfaces

...hardness and conflict do not become something splendid, but a *defect*... Conflict is dissipated...This dissolution eliminates all tensions".

Nietz: "Beethoven composed music above the ["subservient"] heads of...the people...[of] bad taste".

Witt: "Beethoven is a realist through and through; I mean his music is totally true...he sees life totally as it is and then he exalts it...He doesn't lull one into a beautiful dream but redeems the world by viewing it like a hero, as it is". Wittgenstein then fell silent.

Nietz: "Around the hero everything becomes a tragedy".

Philo: "Beethoven's music conveys such a great nobility of spirit, compassionately uplifting one and all; embracing the gay music of village folk, not least the exuberant dancing country bumpkin!

"Also, philosophy as poetry would never be correct or mistaken! There never is any room for tragedy as personal in philosophy, or in science".

Nietz: "I know my fate...I am not a man, I am dynamite...my truth is *dreadful*: for hitherto the lie has been called truth. – [With a] *Revaluation of all values*...I was the first to sense – *smell* – the lie as [objective] lie... I am the first *immoralist*".

"I...understand myself as the first *tragic philosopher*...Before me... *tragic wisdom* was lacking – I have sought in vain for signs of it... Affirmation of transitoriness *and destruction...becoming* with a radical rejection even of the concept '*being*'".

"*I have been the first to discover the tragic*. The Greeks, thanks to their moralistic superficiality, misunderstood it. Even resignation is *not* a lesson of tragedy, but a misunderstanding of it! Yearning for nothingness is a *denial* of tragic wisdom, its opposite!" I quoted Schopenhauer's view against life: "'...life can give no true satisfaction...[so is] not worth our attachment...the tragic spirit...leads to resignation'. Ah, how differently Dionysus spoke to me!"

Philo: "You interpreted tragic wisdom in Dionysian philosophy".

Nietz: Once more, "Dionysus is a philosopher".

Philo: "However, Hesiod's praiseworthy kind of Eris means Strife as not cruel but healthy, courageous and joyful striving for victory. Yet you did not acknowledge that in this way splendid Greek tragic wisdom can begin! Further, you wrote of retracing the – even joyously tragic – singing and dance steps of 'the Dionysian procession from India to Greece', but you were unable to investigate its origin in the cult of Shiva, 'Lord of the Dance'. Also, the expression 'super-man' is even mentioned as *uttara purusha* in the *Chandogya Upanishad* [VIII 12.3]: anticipating being a Shiva-like dancer, emulating the god's serious and joyful dancing over the ego as dwarf demon of Forgetfulness. Most unfortunately, you did not recognize that Shivaism expresses much 'tragic wisdom'. But instead, I understand you see Socrates' tragedy as superseded by your Zarathustra's tragedy, which commences with affirming the latter's sun-like setting".

37

Nietz: "The tragedy begins...[Zarathustra says to the dawning sun:] 'I must descend to the depths, as you do in the evening when you go behind the sea and still bring light to the underworld, you over-rich [or "super-abundant"] star. Like you, I must go under (*untergehen*)'".

Philo: "If I may again interpose here: the Persian Zoroaster, called in Greek 'Zoroastres', the moralist founder of Zoroastrianism, is considered now to have lived in north-east Persian around 1500 BC (and not 600 BC as traditionally thought). He taught the earliest known dualistic Aryan religion: of battle between good deities and evil demons".

Nietz: "Zarathustra was the first to see...[he] *created* this most fateful of errors, morality: consequently he [my Zarathustra as philosopher] must also be the first to *recognize* it...the whole of history is indeed the experimental refutation of...so-called 'moral world-order'".

Philo: "But that which is essentially personal needs to be distinguished from essentially objective refutation, error or correctness".

Nietz: At the very outset of "my 'free thinking'", I believed: "When one has disclosed these methods ["passion, error and self-deception"] to be the foundation of all existing religions and metaphysical systems, one has refuted them". But later I wrote also of "*noble* taste...[wise, calm "victory" over and] above a more passionate current [of heated tradition] running underneath...[thus] I illuminate...this *underworld* of the ideal... One [so-called] error after another is calmly laid on ice, the ideal is not refuted – *it freezes*".

Philo (facing Nietzsche): "It would be most helpful, now, if you could please be so kind as to elaborate on this, your new undertaking".

Nietz: "we stand in need of a *critique* of moral values, *the value of these values*" – "the *value* of morality". Hitherto, "I see nobody who ventured a critique of moral valuations" – "*alone*...I descended into the ["dark"] depths, I tunnelled into the foundations, I commenced an investigation and digging out...to undermine our ["ancient"] *faith in morality*" – proceeding by way of revealing "the fundamental insights into the origins of morality".

Philo: "Yet such language still makes it sound as though your desired moral task was a quite scientific investigation. But please continue".

Nietz: "Strange madness of moral judgments!" – "Madness is something rare in individuals – but in groups, parties, peoples, ages it is the rule" – "supreme value [of the herd]...became master...[because] it was stronger numerically" – "human herds (family groups, communities, tribes, nations, states, churches)...hitherto nothing has been practised and cultivated among men better or longer than obedience...the herd-instinct of obedience" – with its "ideal of a shy, renunciatory, humble, selfless humanity" – "the herd-man...is...useful to the herd".

Philo: "Yet a chorus, teamwork, even two people acting in harmony together can be uplifting for all involved. But again please proceed".

Nietz: "morality itself is a special case of immorality...The declining instincts have become master over the ascending instincts – The will to nothingness has become master over the will to life!" – "Virtue is our greatest misunderstanding". "'Virtue' made completely abstract was the greatest seduction to make oneself abstract: i.e., to detach oneself" – "the serious illness [originated]...enclosed within the [psychological] walls of society ["social organization"]...All instincts which do not discharge themselves outwardly *turn inwards* – this is that which I call the *Verinnerlichung* of man...["forced" to be] turned backwards *against* [individual] *man himself*". Thus "through...violence...a fearful tyranny... of oppression...'bad conscience' developed" – "the 'soul' first develops".

Philo: "– suffering from self, divided against oneself, indivi-duality suffers self-denial".

Nietz: "All human life is sunk deep in untruth" – "the spiritual and psychical nature of man [is] on the whole dark and gloomy". "Man, imprisoned in...[objective] errors, became...sick...full of hatred for the impulses of life, full of mistrust of all that is beautiful and happy in life" – "for thousands of years...human intellect...projected its [objectively] mistaken conceptions...it demands the *abandonment* of our intellect, of our personal will...[Hence] the world is...errors and fantasies".

When following Schopenhauer, I too even wrote of the traditional view of "the saint, in whom the ego is completely melted away and whose life is...a profound feeling of oneness and identity with all living things...the fire of ['selfless'] love in whose light we cease to understand the word 'I' ...beyond our being...as we usually are".

But imprisoned cave-dwellers, "their perpetual bitter resentment of this constraint fills them with volcanic menace...they revenge themselves for their enforced concealment and compelled restraint". "You suffer...and *destroy your own judgment*! Your revenge rebounds upon you yourself when you defame...*distortedly*". By self-despising "asceticism...man takes a real delight in oppressing himself with excessive claims and afterwards idolizing this tyrann[y]".

Philo: "As you emphasize, profoundly, so much traditional 'morality' of fear and vengeful injurious cruelty raises up wickedness, due not least to the extremely misleading ambiguity of fiery fighting spirit, or calm gentle conviction, arising from either courageous strength or cowardly weakness. The great majority of traditional moral evaluations of 'higher' and 'lower' indeed need to be inverted: what is commonly considered of moral necessity to be the way upwards all too often leads downwards!"

Nietz: "Everything hitherto called 'truth' is recognized as the most harmful, malicious, most subterranean form of the [objective] lie...The concept 'the Beyond', 'real world' invented so as to deprive of value the *only* world which exists". "Almost everything we call 'higher culture' is based on...*cruelty*...the 'wild beast'...flourishes...That which constitutes the painful voluptuousness [and "dangerous thrills"] of tragedy is cruelty ...the sufferings of *others*...also...making oneself suffer".

"Art is the great stimulus to life". Even so: "One does not ["better"] understand (*besser verstehen*) the essence (*das Wesen*) of things through art and religion". "The need for...revenge...for lying...which has retreated [or "been repressed"] reappears in the artist" – as "this artistic cruelty, this desire to give a ["beautiful"] form to...suffering...oneself...divided" – "artists...have raised to a heavenly transfiguration precisely those ideas that we now know to be false: artists glorify mankind's religious and philosophical errors, and they could not have done so without believing in their absolute truth".

Philo: "Once more, distinction is needed between personal belief and what is objective".

Nietz: "The artist...believes in gods and demons, instils a soul into nature, hates the sciences...he has halted at [or "still plays"] games that pertain to [earlier: "unreasonableness of"] youth and childhood". At first I wrote that the "*will* in Schopenhauer's sense...[is] opposite of the aesthetic, purely contemplative [so-called] will-less state...the will [as essentially acting] is...not aesthetic". "But now [I see] there is...art as the *good* will to [create] appearance".

Thus there manifests "the cowardice of the 'idealist', who takes flight in the face of reality".

Philo (facing Wittgenstein): "Please now be so kind as to break your prolonged silence on this most keen expression of personal morality, for the philosopher's essential articulation of concepts includes the concept of 'the tragic'".

Witt: "What I do think essential is carrying out the work of clarification with *courage*: otherwise it becomes just a clever game" – "on the barren heights of cleverness".

Nietz: "Reality has been deprived of its value, its [attributed, enhanced personal] meaning...The lie of the ideal has hitherto been the curse on reality...Error (– belief in the ideal –) is not blindness, error is cowardice ...I do not refute ideals, I merely draw on gloves in their presence...above all to *hear* correctly".

Witt: "One might say: 'Genius is talent exercised with courage'". For: "Courage is always original". "Someone who does not lie [without such "clever trick"] is already original enough".

Nietz: "I count nothing more valuable and rare today than honesty".

Witt: "Let me hold on to this that I do not want to deceive myself. That is, a certain demand".

Philo: "And any correctness, mistake, deception or lie is always determined, established as such in some objective practice".

Nietz: "our honesty, our will not to deceive *ourselves*, must prove itself" – "honesty, compels us to deny [traditional] morality".

40

Witt: "a man will never be great if he misjudges himself".

Nietz: "One should not let oneself be misled".

Witt: "Nothing is so difficult as not deceiving oneself".

Nietz: "Honesty...is our [later: "only"] virtue, from which we cannot get free, we free spirits".

"*The free spirit* (*Freigeist*) [is] *a relative concept*...[and] the exception: bound spirits are the rule...the free spirit...has released himself from tradition". From 1876, I wrote "a series [of five books: HH, AOM, WS, D, GS]...whose common goal it is to erect a new image and ideal of the free spirit" – expressing "the *freedom*...our ideal demands...above morality". Thus "I am...[an] immoralist...speaking immorally [or "unmorally"], extra-morally, 'beyond good and evil' (*unmoralisch, aussermoralisch, 'jenseits von Gut und Böse'*)".

Philo: "– which, again, means morality in a sense beyond, higher than traditional good and evil. Please give some further account of your ideal".

Nietz: "during the longest period of the human past nothing was more terrible than to feel that one stood by oneself. To be alone to be an individual" – "polytheism...in some distant overworld (*Überwelt*)...first honoured the rights of individuals. The invention of gods, heroes and overmen (*Übermenschen*) of all kinds, as well as...fairies...and devils... ["permitted"] sovereignty of the individual: the freedom...one eventually granted to oneself" – "for will, as the affect of command, is the decisive sign of sovereignty and strength".

"Perhaps no one has ever been sufficiently truthful about what 'truthfulness' is". Initially, I believed: "There has never yet been an *Übermensch*...I found even the greatest man – all-too-human!' – each lacking, "even the greatest all too human!" – *"Disgust* at mankind is my danger" – to cure which, Zarathustra's animals said, "go out especially to the song-birds, so that you may learn *singing* from them!" And later I wrote, "elevation, advance, strengthening...there are cases of individual success constantly appearing...from the most various cultures in which a *higher type* does manifest itself: something which in relation to collective mankind is a sort of *Übermensch*". By such "higher activity – I mean individual activity...as [a] quite particular, single and unique [person]".

"The discipline of...*great* suffering...alone...has created every elevation of mankind...That tension of the soul in misfortune which cultivates its strength [or "energy"]...inventiveness and bravery...exploiting misfortune ...[by] the hardness of the hammer". "The noble type of man...*creates values*...the noble human being too aids the unfortunate".

"the alchemist...changes something [judged] negligible or contemptible into something of value, even gold. He alone enriches...I've asked myself what mankind has always hated, feared, and despised the most – and precisely out of this I've made my 'gold'" – which also means "alchemy in reverse: the devaluation of what is [reputedly] most valuable".

Witt: "Man's greatest happiness is love".

Nietz: "one stops loving oneself properly when one stops loving others. Which is why the latter is a very bad idea. (I speak from experience.)".

"love acknowledges no power, nothing that separates, differentiates, ranks higher or subordinates [or: "above and below"]'. "That which is done out of love always takes place beyond good and evil" – "the whole concept of 'selfless action', if carefully examined, evaporates into the air ...how *could* he [a man] do anything that had no reference to himself, that is, with no inner compulsion...personal need [earlier: "personal motivation"]?...it is...impossible".

Philo: "Please elaborate on this".

Nietz: "My task...follows of necessity from the insight that...under precisely its [mankind's] holiest value-concepts rather the instinct of denial, of decay, the *décadence* instinct has seductively ruled...the cunningly revengeful...The decisive sign...is...the hostility accorded the egoistic...in a word 'selflessness' – that has hitherto been called *morality*".

"spiritual independence, the will to stand alone...raises the individual above the herd and...is henceforth called *evil*". As briefly stated before [see p.24]: "The free human being is [called] immoral because in all things he is determined to depend upon himself and not upon a tradition: in all the original conditions of mankind, 'evil' signifies the same as 'individual', 'free'...Originally...morality...demanded...the individual is to sacrifice himself...Those [men each creating as]...individual a morality... as a means to his own advantage, as his personal key to happiness, are the exceptions...they [relatively] cut themselves off from the community, as immoral men, and are in the profoundest sense evil" – "called criminals... bad men" – 'the faith preached...that egoism is reprehensible...depriving egoism of its good conscience...Beginning with Socrates, these thinkers ["ancient philosophers" in the West] never wearied of preaching: "Your thoughtlessness and...submission...["to the rule" and another's] opinion is the reason why you so rarely achieve happiness".

Witt: "It's a good thing I don't allow myself to be influenced!" – "Don't take the example of others as your guide, but nature!"

Nietz: "above the...human lowlands there is ["lives"] a *higher, brighter humanity*, very small in number...more solitary" – "we...live on mountains, apart, 'untimely'".

At first it may seem: "One should speak...only of that which one has *overcome*...things that lie *beneath* and *behind* [oneself]". However now "I want to hear your ruling idea, and not that you have escaped from a yoke...Free from what? [My] Zarathustra does not care about that! But your eye should clearly tell me: free for what?"

Nietzsche's Will to Power
– to only Poetic Morality

Nietz: Now I am ultimately "explaining our entire instinctual life as the development and ramification of *one* basic form of will – as will to power, as is *my* theory [or "thesis", *Satz*]" – "the cardinal instinct [or "drive"] of an organic being. A living thing seeks above all to *discharge* its strength – life itself is *Will to Power* [*Wille zur Macht*]" – "the essence of life, its *will to power*" – "the really fundamental instinct of life which aims at the expansion of power...The great and the small struggle always revolves around superiority (*Übergewicht*), around growth and expansion...in accordance with the will to power".

"All great things are the cause of their own destruction, through an act of self-cancellation: the law of life, the law of *necessary* self-overcoming which is the essence of life, wills it".

Philo: "Healthy and noble individual life certainly demands growth, for greater strength, which means relative continual wilful striving to surpass, to improve oneself".

Nietz: "To refrain from mutual injury, mutual violence, mutual exploitation...[is] good manners [or "conduct"]...[when] individuals [should] treat one another as equals...[Nonetheless] life itself is essentially [amoral] appropriation, injury, overpowering of the strange and weaker, suppression...exploitation...life *is* will to power...as a reality [so called] it is the *primordial* [or "*fundamental*"] *fact* of all history" – "life operates essentially...through injury, violation, exploitation and destruction" – "in real life it is only a question of *strong and weak wills*".

"for will to come into being an idea of pleasure and displeasure is needed...[that] depends on the interpretation of the intellect". "'Willing' is not 'desiring', striving, demanding: it is distinguished from these by the affect of commanding". "Willing liberates: for willing is creating".

Philo: "Again, willing creates and destroys, so liberates or enslaves. An individual's chosen acts of freewill show commanding strength of some complete independence. For the will and understanding must accompany each other in anyone's practice, as conceptually so called; willing always involves some consciousness of acting".

Nietz: "in every act of will there is a ruling thought...who *wills* commands...[and] renders obedience [or "obeys"]...we are at the same time the commanding *and* the obeying parties" – "the commander... commands himself: then also must...practice obedience ["obey himself"] even in commanding" – "know morality as a continual [relative] self-command and self-overcoming practised" – "ever increasing elevation".

Thus "this first outburst of...self-determination...this will to *free* will". "It is not a matter of going ahead (...[as a leader,] a herdsman...), but of being able *to go it alone*, of being able *to be different*".

"But this loneliness, ever since childhood! This reserve, in the most intimate relationships!...basically I think that no one can help me overcome this deep-rooted feeling of being alone" – "if I didn't sense the enormous fertility of my new philosophy, I'd begin to feel horribly isolated".

Philo: "Writing books certainly aims to reach out to – and in some way to help inspire – other people".

Nietz: "Am I a philosopher? Who cares?"

Witt: Likewise: "May it [my *Philosophical Investigations*] soon...be completely forgotten by the philosophical journalists" – "from the bottom of my heart it is all the same to me what the professional philosophers of today think of me; for it is not for them that I am writing".

Philo: "The dawning great insight that freedom from oppressive widespread tradition is by ever-higher, noble, healthy strength of independence of embodied spirit, surely means rising above feeling isolated".

Nietz: This relative "spiritual freedom" means, time after time, "a victory – an overcoming of *oneself* which has to be communicated for the benefit of others" – so "everyone goes away...richer in himself...full of a new will and current".

Philo: "Swimming relatively independently through life, not only with the currents".

Nietz: "Everyone has his good days, when he finds [or creates] his higher self".

And at the start of "my 'free thinking'", I stated a main insight that "the world is not good and not evil" – "good...beautiful...evil...we impose such words upon things [perceived] external to and within us" – "men have given themselves all their good and evil".

Witt: To repeat, in like manner: "What is good and evil is essentially the I, not the world". "Good and evil only enter through the subject...the willing subject".

Nietz: "Thus the question...[arises]: *Why have morality at all* when life, nature, and history [themselves] are 'not moral'?" – "In the great silence... sea...sky...cliffs...none of them can speak...this silent [judged] beauty...is a deception [objectively]...[which would] teach man to cease to be man! Shall he surrender to you? Shall he become as you...mute...?" – "You desire to *live* 'according to Nature'?...what fraud of words! Imagine... a being...boundlessly indifferent, without purpose or consideration [or: "aims or intentions"]...To live – is not that just endeavouring [or "desiring"] to be otherwise than this Nature?" – "no longer like a leaf in the wind, a plaything of absurdity, of the absence of meaning...[but] to *will* something".

Philo: "Each human person essentially belongs to that part of Nature which expresses more or less rational and so moral freewill. Allowing the insentient to rule entirely would mean the living choosing to be stupefied, dead; living must mean some ongoing willing, desiring, valuing, choosing creatively to become".

Nietz: For "nothing is valuable 'in itself'".

Philo: "Yet that correctly denies Absolute Objectivity, not relativity!"

Nietz: "To divide the world into a 'real' and an 'apparent' world...is only...a symptom of a *declining* life" – "the 'real' world has only been *lyingly added*" – "the thing-in-itself...is...[not merely unknowable but] empty of meaning". The "world as idea, that is, as [objective] error". "We have abolished ["the longest error"] the real world...*we have also abolished the apparent world*".

Witt: Certainly: "The meaning of a word is no longer for us an object corresponding to it".

Philo: "The metaphysical tradition via Kant mistakenly claimed dual worlds of reality in itself appearing represented as phenomena. Plainly not everything is merely language, but still the idea of reality said to be always beyond all language remains a fiction of language".

Nietz: The question to be answered now is: "the apparent *objective* character of things: could it not be merely a difference of degree ["that which changes slowly"] within the subjective?"

"the ascetic morality of depersonalization" – "depersonalization of the spirit...[means] objective man...no longer...dealing with *his troubles*" – that is "the cult of 'objectivity'". "All experiences are moral experiences, even in the realm of sense perception". "'Objectivity' in the philosopher [and the scientist means]: moral indifference toward oneself". "It is the intellect's ambition to seem no longer to belong to an individual". Even further, "art 'for its own sake'...and 'pure knowledge'...[express] disgust with oneself".

"Therefore: either no will – the hypothesis of science – or free will" – "science...constitutes not the opposite of the ascetic ideal but rather its most recent and most refined form...a hiding-place" – "knowledge [means]...something familiar...so that we no longer marvel at it".

Witt: Here I may at least ask: "is it...noticing for the first time these things ["birth, sickness, death...dreams", rather like Siddhartha Gautama, and being]...understandably amazed?...Man has to awaken to wonder... Science is a way of sending him to sleep again".

Nietz: "belief in the ascetic ideal...is the belief in a *metaphysical* value, the value of *truth* [claimed 'found'] *in itself*...there is absolutely no science 'without presuppositions'...a 'belief' must always exist first in order for science to derive from it a direction...a method...science itself *requires* justification (which is not to say that such justification exists)...the will to truth itself first requires justification". "This unconditional will to truth...

the [later: "metaphysical"] faith in science...does *not* mean 'I will not allow myself to be deceived [objectively]' but – there is no alternative – 'I will not deceive, not even myself'; and with that we stand on moral ground".

"Ultimately, man finds in things nothing but what he himself has imported". "Man first implanted values into things...he created the meaning of things, a human meaning!...Valuating is itself...the jewel of all valued things...without evaluation the nut of existence would be hollow".

Philo: "But it has to be said, once more, that the world so called is always relatively and never Absolutely in human terms; any other than human meaning is only to some extent like or unlike human meaning".

Nietz: Early on I affirmed that: "In becoming everything is hollow, [objectively] deceptive, shallow and worthy of our contempt...[and that judgment means such a] human being despises his happiness and his unhappiness". But "perverse wizards...create nothing out of the world" – in a "mysticism, [of] the voluptuous enjoyment of eternal emptiness" – like "the teacher of the religion of self-redemption, the Buddha".

Philo: "You spoke before of "the risk of longing for a Buddha-like denial of the will" and "yearning for the Void" [see p.10]. Yet it should be made clear that originally Buddhist teaching, the *dharma*, actually proclaims no self, no religious belief, no teaching, no universe, that is universal extinction called *nirvana*!

"If I may say a little more on this (no-)teaching: the *dharma* mistreats and misjudges all the world as only illusory and evil causal appearance, empty dualities of fated necessary self-opposition: all being is no-being. It means to be completely self-contradictory, self-defeating, no-*dharma*! For the *dharma* admits, having appeared to dispel all as dark ignorance, it too must be false and abandoned – but it gives entirely wrong reasons, even causes for this dual, conceptual and moral, necessity. The *dharma* is extreme ascetic pseudo-science against all life; and again differences are other than only oppositions. Clearly, this teaching, as selfless, proclaims no religious faith, no spiritual belief. However, the *dharma* in claiming no belief is still essentially conceptual expression. But it is a too simple, thoroughly misleading, completely mistaken conceptual view – that is the real philosophy of Buddhism!" [See References for further details.]

"And now, if we three all agree, I think it would be most timely and helpful to hear some account of how your view, Nietzsche, of the world as 'moral poem' developed, having shifted from earlier claimed emphasis of only art, and in contrast to traditional ascetic ideals, before we continue with our more interweaving discussion".

Following a brief silence, Nietzsche proceeded:

"The meaninglessness of suffering, and *not* suffering as such, has been the curse which has hung over mankind up to now – *and the ascetic ideal offered mankind a meaning* ["man was *saved*"]!...It *explained* suffering;

46

and it seemed to fill the gaping void...The explanation – there is no doubt – brought new suffering...of *guilt*".

To "reduce the physical world to an illusion, as the [Indian] ascetics of Vedanta philosophy did, along with pain, diversity, the whole conceptual opposition of 'subject' and 'object' – [objective] errors, nothing but errors! ...to deny one's own 'reality' – what a triumph! –...a cruel violation of *reason*...ascetic self-contempt, the self-mockery of reason decrees: 'A realm of truth and freedom *does exist*, but reason is the very thing which is excluded from it!'"

"willing directed by the ascetic ideal actually expresses in its entirety: this hatred of the human...of the animal, of the material, this revulsion from the senses, from reason itself, this fear of happiness and beauty, this yearning to pass beyond all appearance, change, becoming, death, desire, beyond yearning itself. All this represents...a *will to nothingness*, an aversion to life, a rebellion...but which is and remains none the less a *will*!" – "human will...*must have a goal* – and it would even will *nothingness* rather than *not* will at all". "He who despises himself still nonetheless respects himself as one who despises".

Thus "the actual facts of the [interpreted] matter: *the ascetic ideal is derived from...instincts of a degenerating life*, which seeks to preserve itself...it points to a partial physiological inhibition and fatigue...The ascetic priest embodies the desire for another existence...But...this desire ...binds him to this life".

Philo: "Again, I should interpose here that even the Buddhist *dharma*, claiming neither ideal nor Absolute Ideal, still holds *nirvana* as the most extreme, unrealizable, ascetic Ideal of universal self-denial, permanent Extinction of all – lastly itself.

"And, if I may briefly add, nihilistic statements are self-defeating in actual practice; senselessly disregarding their objectively certain defined meanings. To deny meaning is essentially to affirm negative meaning. The nihilist would annihilate all meaning, claiming no belief or value, that is self-contradictory belief in nothing, willing nothingness. Affirming 'All is meaningless' essentially expresses cowardly wilful contempt for life.

"But now please kindly continue".

Nietz: "Is meaning not necessarily relative meaning and perspective? All meaning is will to power (all relative meaning resolves itself into it)" – "life itself is *determined* [or *"conditioned"*, *bedingt*] by perspective" – *"perspective* – the fundamental condition – of life". "The [individual's] will to power *interprets*...value". "Will to truth is a making firm, a making true...'Truth' is therefore not something...found or discovered – but...must be created...an active determining...Man projects...the world".

"I consider *life itself instinct* for growth...where the will to power is lacking there is decline. My assertion is that this will is *lacking* in all the supreme values of mankind...under the holiest names". For instead:

"The higher human being...is really [or "properly", *eigentliche*] the poet who keeps creating this life...the whole eternally growing world of evaluations...perspectives, scales...This poem that we have invented is continually studied by the so-called practical human beings (our actors) who learn their roles and translate everything into flesh and actuality, into the everyday. Whatever has value in our world now does not have value in itself, according to its nature – nature is always value-less, but has been given value...and it was we who gave and bestowed it. Only we have created the world that concerns man! – But precisely this knowledge we lack...we occasionally catch it for a fleeting moment".

Philo: "How could there be nothing genuine about all actors? For every person who lives naturally expresses some sure embodied behavioural acts. Further, Nature as so called is never absolutely completely without value, Void or Valuelessness – that indeed expresses self-mockery of reason. Once more, Nature is always defined relatively in itself as factual kind of objectivity".

Nietz: The "sorcerer" laments: "I am banished from all truth, Only a fool! Only a poet!" – "Only a poet!...That must [objectively] lie...merely speaking colourfully...on deceptive word-bridges...*exiled from all truth! Only fool! Only poet!*"

Philo: "All aesthetic meaning is personal evaluation in poetic language. But surely too, any poetic truth, tale or statement must be able to be also stated roughly in plain unpoetic language".

Witt: Yet still, "a poem, even though it is composed in the language of information, is not used in...giving information".

Philo: "– nor in giving objective description. But again how could one live only as a stuttering poet creating all the world as poem? To repeat, the poet is free to dream or interpret, but never is objective, never is correct and never lies. Also, any metaphorical terms must be objectively defined in practice. Accordingly no one is only a poet, including only a moral poet – even exiled from merely imagined reality absolutely entirely in itself! Not all relative truth, of objective as well as subjective realities, can be genuinely denied".

Nietz: "We have *created* the world that possesses values!" – "a 'free spirit'...cares nothing for what is fixed [by us]...the whole of nature...[is] merely...a metaphor" – "this life...poem that we have invented".

The Philosopher's Task
of Twofold Necessity

Nietz: "Every word is a prejudice" – "a moral prejudice" – "every morality...is a protracted constraint...*obedience* in *one* direction... something for the sake of which it is worthwhile to live on earth, for example, virtue, art, music, dance, reason, spirituality...Protracted unfreedom [or "long bondage"] of spirit, mistrustful constraint in the communicability of ideas...".

Witt: "Nothing is more difficult than facing concepts *without prejudice*. (And that is the principal difficulty of philosophy.)". "One cannot guess how a word functions. One has to *look at* its use and learn from that. But the difficulty is to remove the prejudice which stands in the way of doing this. It is not a *stupid* prejudice".

Philo: "Prejudice is always some more or less harmful personal feeling, or opinion, expressing like or dislike; it can even be mistaken or lying obstruction, that veils, hides or stops – but as personal never falsifies – recognition of some objective certainty, which includes conceptual kinds of known definitions".

Nietz: "The will to power can manifest itself only against resistances" – "all expansion, incorporation, growth means striving against something that resists".

Witt: "Difficulty of philosophy [is] not the intellectual difficulty of the sciences, but the difficulty of a change of attitude (*Umstellung*). Resistances of the will must be overcome" – "the conflict [or "contrast", *Gegensatz*] between the right [correct] understanding...and what most people *want* to see...What has to be overcome is not a difficulty of the understanding but of the will".

Nietz: "philosophy is this tyrannical impulse [or "drive"] itself, the most spiritual (*geistigste*) Will to Power" – "real [or "proper", *eigentlicher*] *power* of spirituality, real *depth* of spiritual insight, in short [means] philosophy".

Witt: "How small a thought it takes to fill someone's whole life!" – "In the [so-called] theories and battles of philosophy we find words whose meanings are well-known to us from everyday life used in an ultra-physical [metaphysical] sense" – "we are dazzled by the ideal and therefore fail to see the actual".

Philo: "– which in comparison is then found dissatisfying. And isn't it true that people may experience their dreams of something as universally fundamental, and also imaginary characters, more intensely, as more real than everyday life?"

Witt: "It is not in practical life that we encounter philosophical problems...it is when we start constructing sentences not for practical purposes". "It is only in normal cases that the use of a word is clearly prescribed; we know, are in no doubt, what to say in this or that case. The more abnormal the case, the more doubtful it becomes what we are to say".

"Philosophers are often like little children who scribble...Adults have often drawn something for the child and said: 'That is a man', 'That is a house' and so on. So now the child draws lines and asks: 'What's that?'" – "'philosophy'...[is] the activity of pointing out such [linguistic] mistakes" – "we are tempted...to talk nonsense...and then ask...questions [which] are illegitimate. We solve the puzzle by giving the correct grammatical rules". "The problems ["in philosophy"] are dissolved in the actual sense of the word – like a lump of sugar in water" – "the [arising] philosophical problems should *completely* disappear".

Philo: "In correct philosophy there is nothing to justify, question, doubt or think! Philosophy correctly only describes objectively certain sense or senselessness in practice. Strictly, any questioning of objective certainty is always senseless; concepts as such, as with knowledge itself, cannot be genuinely doubted. And arising philosophical thoughts, that is, claims to think sense or senselessness, are essentially unrealizable misconceptions. This means all speculative philosophy is metaphysical mistake, that is, imaginative thought making false claims to objectivity.

"Accordingly too, however, philosophical problems or questions are not all metaphysical pitfalls, or merely idle misunderstandings of thought. The ongoing – and in a practical sense genuine – objective problems of philosophy ask for further articulation, for sufficiently explicit descriptive conceptual rules of sense, and not only senselessness, made in practice".

Witt: Indeed, "in philosophy...our work...has no end". "What *we* [philosophers need to] do is to bring words back from their metaphysical to their ["original home" of] everyday use". "It is not our aim to refine or complete the system of rules for the use of our words in unheard-of ways".

Nietz: "To employ innovations or quaint old terms in language, to favour the rare and strange...is always a sign of an immature or corrupted taste. A noble poverty, [in contrast is] but a masterly freedom within this unpretentiousness...with the everyday".

Witt: "What's ragged [or "fuzzy"] should be left ragged [description]".

Nietz: "Just as the good prose-writer employs only words that belong to common speech...so the good poet of the future will depict only reality [as interpreted] and completely ignore all those fantastic, superstitious... subjects...[of] earlier poets".

Witt: "In philosophy there is no need to use new words; the old familiar ["straight-forward"] words of the language are quite sufficient".

Nietz: "Their [philosophers' understanding or] thinking is, in fact, far less a discovery than a re-recognizing, a remembering".

Witt: "Learning philosophy really *is* a remembering. We remind ourselves that we have really used words in this way".

Philo: "And a particular word often has very different meanings, which allows creation of much confusion – as well as humour!"

Witt: "Grammar tells us what kind of object anything is". "We remind ourselves...of the *kind of statement* that we make about phenomena...Our investigation is therefore a grammatical one. Such an investigation sheds light on our problem by clearing ["the fog" of] misunderstandings away".

Nietz: Indeed, "metaphysics...might sound...befogging". "Perspectival seeing is the *only* kind of seeing there is, perspectival 'knowing' the *only* kind of 'knowing'; and the *more* feelings about a matter which...come to expression...the more complete our 'conception' of it, our 'objectivity' will be. But to eliminate the will completely, to suspend the feelings altogether...would this not amount to the *castration* of the intellect?"

Philo: "But how can objectivity itself be rooted in personal sentiment?"

Witt: "What has a soul, or pain, to do with a stone?...How could one so much as get the idea of ascribing a *sensation* [or will] to a *thing*...[or] a number!" Also: "Our attitude to what is alive and to what is dead, is not the same. All our reactions are different".

Nietz: I have continued to maintain that we "have a *moral* origin" – "led by instinctive moral definitions".

Philo: "Bewitched into trusting Circe!"

Nietz: "Of decisive importance [is that]: behind all other evaluations these moral evaluations stand in command".

"To remain objective, hard, firm, severe in carrying through an idea – artists succeed best in this". "One seeks [to create] a...philosophy in which...we feel freest; i.e., in which our most powerful drive feels free to function" – "authentic instinct for life most unconditionally posits truth".

Witt: "what is the use of studying philosophy...if it does not improve your thinking about the important questions of everyday life?"

Philo: "– by improving recognition of conceptual practice. Feeling and thinking of – even best – certainty never guarantees that which is believed to be the case. Morality as essentially personal never defines any rules".

Nietz: "faith in reason...is...moral".

Witt: "Philosophy unties knots ["entanglement in our rules"] in our thinking; hence its result must be simple, but philosophizing has to be as complicated as the ["false and oversimplified" – such as "noun, adjective and verb"] knots it unties".

Nietz: "the most valuable insights are *methods*".

Witt: "All I can give you is a method". "I myself still find my way of philosophizing new...This method consists essentially in leaving the question of *truth* and asking about *sense* instead".

Philo: "And that means, in other more explicit words: philosophy only describes various conceptual kinds of sense of senselessness in objective practice, and never concerns known particular reference as such, which is only supplied by science. For all definition is both sense and reference".

Witt: "I know that my method is right...I want my [statements of] philosophy...to get something settled".

Philo: "If I may also add the reminder here: thinking or feeling never settles anything decisively, but objective conceptual recognition does!"

Witt: "confusion...considers a philosophical problem as though...[it] concerned a [contingent] fact of the world". "We want to replace wild conjectures and explanations by quiet weighing of linguistic facts".

Philo: "– calm noting of relatively necessary conceptual kinds of statements made, given in practice".

Witt: "*Essence* is expressed by grammar". "The rules of grammar are independent of the [particular known] facts".

Nietz: "grammar (the metaphysics of the people)".

Philo: "Surely there is no greater philosophical blunder!"

Witt: It is "the herd which has created this language" – "the grammar of our ordinary language...is already there".

Nietz: "'It is given' – that is also a doctrine of submission" – "to let oneself be determined by one's environment is decadent".

Witt: "the task of philosophy is not to create a new, ideal language, but to clarify the use of our language, the existing language".

Nietz: "The philosophical objective outlook can therefore be a sign that will and strength are small...'men of knowledge', who desire only to ascertain what is, are those who cannot *fix* anything *as it ought to be* ...who leave everything as it is".

Witt: "Philosophy may in no way interfere with the actual use of language; it can in the end only describe it. For it cannot give it any foundation either. It leaves everything as it is".

Nietz: "creative positing...overcoming, willing...is of the essence of philosophy. To introduce a meaning – this task still remains...; that is, active interpretation and not merely conceptual translation".

Philo: "Interpretation? The philosopher's descriptions compare and distinguish to make more explicit different kinds of sense or senseless in practice, thereby certainly creating some new conceptual connections. And the philosopher only describes conceptually and never knows; only the scientist knows. Science and philosophy constitute the two main objective, relatively entirely different, kinds of rational practice".

Witt: "philosophical problems...are solved [or "dissolved" - see p.50], not by giving new information". "Philosophy...neither explains nor deduces anything. – Since everything lies open to view there is nothing to explain". Going "through the thicket of questions out into the open" – "nothing is concealed...nothing is hidden".

Nietz: The contrast concerns "merely a believer and not one who first *creates* truth" – "where one did not know how to explain one learned to create" – "philosophers...must no longer accept concepts as a gift...but first *make* and *create* them" – "this task itself demands...[they] *create values*".

"Actual philosophers [those who are "genuinely philosophical"]...are commanders and law-givers" – "they reach for the future with creative hand, and everything...becomes for them a means, an instrument, a hammer. Their 'knowing' is *creating*, their creating is a law-giving". "He who *determines* values and directs the will...giving direction to the highest natures is the *highest* man" – through "exercise of...the art of commanding".

Philo: "The needed skilful art of philosophy, as really objective and in addition moral, itself is never knowledge or aesthetic".

Nietz: "*new philosophers*...[need to] teach man the future of man as his *will*...a revaluation of values". So, for example, as to my book *Twlight of the Idols*: "Its meaning in four words: revaluation of all values" – "the task of the philosopher dawns: the determination of value" – "the future task of the philosopher:..[is] the determination of the *hierarchy of values*".

Philo: "Concepts as always descriptive remain on the same objective level: that is to say, unjustifiable, underivable from one another, and also amoral. The philosopher as objective needs no ladder, never goes up or down. Even so, it is surely clear enough, from what you have each said, that the philosopher's task is a twofold necessity of objective conceptual descriptions and personal moral evaluations. Human nature is inherently more or less strongly wilful, rational and thereby moral or immoral. Any rational person must morally select subjective and objective phenomena. Actions of individuals, even as relatively impersonal philosophers and scientists, to some extent – which never compromises objectivity itself – also need to be guided by personal choices. We morally must choose to make valuations, wilfully guiding actions, for any ongoing improvement. Accordingly, the philosopher of twofold 'right necessity' articulates some objective sense or senselessness of objective and moral imperatives.

"Philosophy as itself only conceptual description is never hierarchical. Philosophy of morality correctly only describes some objective sense, or senselessness, of statements of personal moral hierarchical perspectives. Moral judgments, or valuations – misleadingly called 'determinations' – are always creations of higher or lower, better or worse, subjective values amorally defined. Justification as moral is never objective knowledge, and never correct or mistaken, but merely attempts personal persuasion.

(facing Nietzsche) "And so, if what you declare of 'the philosopher' is taken, in an objective sense, to mean only 'the philosopher as moral', that is, conveying conceptual descriptions of moral values, then we can clearly proceed to hear your moral philosophy and evaluate it in due course".

Nietz: "The development of reason is adjustment [or "adaption"], invention, with the aim of making similar, equal [or "identical"]...[for] only when we see things coarsely [or "crudely"] and made equal do they become calculable and usable to us" – "all life is based on appearance, art, [objective] deception...the necessity of perspective and error".

"The [objective] falseness of an opinion [or "judgment"] is not for us any objection to it: it is here, perhaps, that our new language sounds most strangely. The question is, how far an opinion [or "judgment"] is life-furthering, life-preserving...we...maintain that the falsest opinions are...the most indispensable to us; that without a recognition of logical fictions... purely *imagined*...counterfeiting [or objective "falsification"] of the world by means of numbers, man could not live...To recognize untruth as a condition of life:...[such] a philosophy...has thereby alone placed itself beyond good and evil".

Philo: "Your new moral philosophy is 'beyond good and evil' of the whole of traditional morality".

Nietz: "We sail straight over morality and *past* it" – with "a feeling of birdlike freedom, birdlike perspective". "One must have liberated oneself from many things that oppress, inhibit, hold down, and make heavy" – that is "the abyss, the Spirit of Gravity, my devil [as "dwarf"]...leaden thoughts...abysmal thought...[so too] a heavy black snake...[in the] mouth ...throat".

Philo: "– which symbolizes all dark vision, hardness and bitterness of heart".

Nietz: "I would not know what the spirit of a philosopher might wish more to be than a good dancer" – having "intellectual *light feet*...being able to dance with concepts, with words". Yet, once again, as: "Only a poet...speaking colourfully".

Philo: "So I understand that the moral philosopher can be described as needing the "*light* feet" of a skilful dancing poet; not heavy, fixed and awkward, but with flexible and graceful body, feet and hands – even like the most striking portrayal of Shiva's serious and joyful dancing over the dwarf demon of Forgetful selfishness".

Nietz: "What a philosopher is, is hard to learn, because it cannot be taught...and all popular conceptions of them are [objectively] false. Thus, for example, that genuinely philosophical...dialectical severity and necessity which never takes a false step". Thus also "the real [or "proper", *eigentlichen*] antithesis – the *degenerated* instinct which turns against life with subterranean vengefulness...and...*supreme affirmation*...even of suffering...boundlessly exuberant Yes to life" – comprehending "denial *and destruction* is a condition of affirmation".

"I contradict as has never been contradicted and am none the less the opposite of a negative spirit". "He [my Zarathustra] contradicts with every word, this the most affirmative of all spirits; all opposites are in him bound together into a new unity". "My style [in TSZ] is a dance; it plays with all sorts of symmetries, only to leap over and scoff at [or "mock"] them" – "thought...[is] a closest relation of high spirits and the dance!"

Philo: "Your Zarathustra in merely mocking dialectics is still caught in dialectics!"

Nietz: "I am suspicious [or "mistrustful"] of dialectics, even of reasons. More important, it seems to me, is courage...I myself have only rarely the courage of [or "to affirm"] what I know". "The general imprecise way of observing sees everywhere in nature opposites (as, e.g., 'warm and cold') where there are, not opposites, but differences of degree...transitions".

Phio: "But talking in merely dialectical terms still does not express any other, new language, despite your having recognized actually only degrees of difference".

Nietz: "What strange simplification and falsification mankind lives in! ...*language* cannot get over its coarseness and continues to speak of antitheses where there are only degrees...to hold us in this *simplified*, altogether artificial, fabricated, falsified world".

Philo: "And that conveys a very important genuine objective insight. For as Wittgenstein eventually also recognized, and most helpfully made sufficiently clear in public, conceptual sense describes actually dynamic, incomplete essences of everyday meanings. Accordingly, any philosophy of our ordinary language as dialectics is thoroughly but too obsessively confrontational, that is, misleadingly oppositional. The entire dialectical tradition of philosophy is oversimplified mistaken ideal, casting a long dark shadow of too sharply delineated deception! Contrast, as between self and otherness, is more than only completely contra, for and against. Difference remains different to being always contradictory. Even denial or negation is other than only complete opposition to affirmation".

Witt: Now "my interest is in showing that things which look the same are really different. I was thinking of using as a motto for my book [*Philosophical Investigations*] a quotation from *King Lear*: 'I'll teach you differences'".

To repeat, everyday "sense" is not "sharply bounded" – but means "a concept with blurred edges". "Many words...don't have a strict meaning. But this is not a defect...[likewise a] real light...has no sharp boundary".

Nietz: "our *humanization* – a genuine and actual *progress* –...[means] no opposites at all – we may love the senses, we have spiritualized and made them artistic in every degree" – "shadow is as needful as light. They are not opponents: they stand, rather, lovingly hand in hand".

Philo: "And, I should like to say, that reminds me of the Greek creation myth relating Hemera (Day) was born of Nyx (Night), Erebus (Darkness), Eros (Desire) and in the beginning Chaos".

Introspection
as Essentially Defined

Nietz: "I am no seeker. I want to create for myself". And yet: "No, life has not disappointed me...I find it...[now too as] seeker for knowledge [or "the knower", *des Erkennenden*] – and...not trickery (*eine Betrügerei*) ...'Life as a means to knowledge' – with this principle in one's heart one can live not only boldly but even gaily" – "there exists a downright cult of suffering...[but] to ward it off – 'gay science'".

Philo: "This seems to be in contrast to you earlier dark view that the world is an inescapable "prison" of "lies and deception (*Lug und Trug*)... the basis of all our judgments and 'knowledge'". But you have now made clear that your claim to science is only as moral artist! More specifically, only ever poetic interpretation, perspective, wilfully and imaginatively creating, projecting belief, even as all so-called knowledge or proof".

Nietz: Thus "we...deny the ["ascetic"] ideal...[of] a completely different form of existence...[which "*demands*...life"] somehow turns itself against itself, *denies itself*...The ascetic treats life as a wrong track...a mistake... one *should* rectify...For an ascetic life is a contradiction in terms".

And so "psychology shall again be recognized as the queen of the sciences, to serve and prepare for which the other sciences exist. For psychology is now once again the road to the fundamental problems".

Even so, I may add having expressed that: "My life is now governed by the wish that things are *not* as I see them, and that someone will [objectively] refute my 'truths'" – although a little later I also wrote: "I want to be right not for today or tomorrow but for millennia".

Witt: "My investigation will not be psychological, even though a sentence is in a sense dead until it is understood...One might say it has meaning only for an understanding being. If there were no one to understand the signs we would not call the signs language".

Philo: "The philosopher's statements made, which include remarks on psychology, are genuinely always objective unjustifiable conceptual descriptions, never science, theory, knowledge, proof or refutation".

Nietz: "the spell of definite [or "certain", *bestimmter*] grammatical functions is in the last resort the spell of *physiological* value judgments [or "valuations"]". "The body and physiology the starting point:...feeling, willing, thinking" – "for what does one at present believe in more firmly than in [the "securest possession" of] one's body?" – "we *have* nothing but [will,] thought and sensation".

However, to suppose "sound method demands that we start from the 'inner world', from the 'facts of consciousness', because this world is more familiar to us. Error of errors!" – "Life is...will to power, which, working from within, incorporates and subdues more and more of that which is [merely projected as] 'outside'" – "the essential thing in the [organic] life process is precisely the tremendous shaping, form-creating force [of will] working from within which *utilizes* and *exploits* 'external circumstances'" – "as will to power, as will to deception".

Philo: "It has to be said that your perspective most confusingly claims to interpret all life as objective error, created from the instinctual origin of only deceptive will to power; starting from solely 'working from within' the body, not through more or less conscious kinds of wilful behaviour!"

Nietz: "In every judgment there resides the...belief in subject and attribute [or "predicate"], or in cause and effect...that every activity presupposes an agent". "The separation of the 'deed' from the 'doer', of the event from someone who produces events, of the process from a something...enduring [also: "constant", "being"]...this ancient mythology established...[our] language and grammar". "But...there is no 'being' behind doing, acting, becoming; 'the doer' is merely a fiction imposed on the doing...it posits the same event once as cause and then once again as effect".

Philo: "That sounds just like the Buddha's teaching of no-self and only apparent causality! For that view of 'no-self' [in Sanskrit *anatman*, Pali *anatta*], claiming no selfish 'I', ego or individual, is given in the second sermon seemingly to the five ascetics, called 'The Marks of Non-Soul'".

Witt: "The words 'soul' and 'mind' have been used as though they stood for a thing, a gaseous thing. 'What *is* the soul?' is a misleading question" – "we then look for...an ethereal object".

Philo: "– an ever elusive so-called 'subtle body', a fictitious 'ego-substance'".

Nietz: "'Subject', 'object', 'attribute' [or 'predicate'] – these distinctions are fabricated and...imposed...The fundamental [objectively] false observation is that I believe it is *I* who do something...'have' something" – "the fictitious insertion of a subject". "Subject, object, a doer added to the doing...is...nothing real [itself]" – "it is only relations that constitute an essence" – "thingness has only been invented by us...with the aim of defining, communication".

Witt: To repeat: "what more can I do...Isn't what you reproach me of as though you said: 'In your language you're only *speaking*!'"

Nietz: "we see ourselves...*necessitated* to error, to precisely the extent that our prejudice in favour of reason compels us to posit unity, identity, duration, substance, cause, materiality, being...The situation is the same as with the motions of the sun: in that case error has our eyes, in the present case our *language* as a perpetual advocate".

Witt: "Well, what would it have looked like if it had *looked* as if the earth turned on its axis?" [For fuller quote see References.]

Nietz: "Language...*reason*...sees everywhere deed and doer...believes in will as cause...and...*projects* its belief in the ego-substance...only thus does it *create* the concept 'thing'...it is only from the conception 'ego' that there follows, derivatively, the concept 'being'...the error of being...every word, every sentence we utter speaks in its favour!" – "the conception of ...the ego (the 'subject') as cause...[is] a fable, a fiction...Man projected his...will, spirit, ego, outside himself...he posited 'things' as possessing being according to his own image" – "our 'ego' concept – our oldest article of faith".

Witt: "The word 'I' is one symbol among others having a *practical* use ...It does not stand out among all other words we use in practical life".

Philo (facing Nietzsche): "Claimed fundamental privileging of 'I' over all other meanings is conceptual mistake. Again, concepts are always on the same descriptive level, never hierarchically derived from each other".

Nietz: "The *causa sui* [cause or condition of its own] is the best self-contradiction [later: "nonsense" or "folly"] hitherto imagined...the desire to bear the whole and sole responsibility for one's actions and to absolve ...society from responsibility for them...It is *we* alone who have fabricated causes, succession, reciprocity, relativity, compulsion, number, law, freedom, motive, purpose".

Some still "believe 'immediate certainties' exist, for example, 'I think' [Descartes] or, as was Schopenhauer's superstition, 'I will'...But...when I analyse...'I think' I acquire a series of rash assertions...that it is *I* who think, that it has to be something at all which thinks...as a cause...that I *know* what thinking is"

"thinking...invented the 'ego'". Objectively "it is a *falsification*...to say: the subject 'I' is the condition of the predicate 'think'. *It* thinks... The inference here is...habit of grammar". "'There is thinking: therefore there is something that thinks': that is the upshot of all Descartes' argumentation...our grammatical custom that adds a doer to every deed".

Witt: "It seems as though...that to me...something applied which does not apply to other people. That is...an asymmetry...["absurd" preferential] temptation to use the word 'ego'": "to say...'I *am* in a favoured position. I am the centre of the world'" – or "Descartes' emphasis on 'I'".

"Instead of saying 'I think' or 'I have an ache' one might say 'It thinks' ...[And likewise:] The solipsist who says 'Only my experiences are real' ...Getting into the solipsistic mood means not using the word 'I' in describing a personal experience. Acceptance of such a change is tempting because the description of a sensation does not contain a ["necessary"] reference to either a person [or "a body"] or a sense organ ...no person necessarily comes into it...its being *mine* is not essential to its description...It is an experiential proposition that an eye sees".

Philo: "In other words, any description of perception only contingently – not objectively necessarily – refers to a possessor, to being possessed".

Witt: Furthermore: "'I am...' Now in saying this I don't name any [one] person". "'I' is not the name of a person". The solipsist in saying "'when anything is seen, it is always I who see'...did not wish to point to a particular ['I']...The idea that he had made a significant statement arose from a confusion" – "it is the particular use of a word only which gives the word its meaning...we recognize a particular person by his bodily characteristics" – "that it makes sense to suppose that I change my body, but that it does not make sense to suppose that I have a self without a body, shows that the word 'I' cannot be replaced by 'this body'; and...that 'I' only has meaning with reference to a [changeable] body. A parallel in chess is that although the king is not to be identified with this piece of wood, at the same time one cannot talk of a pure king of chess which has no mark or symbol corresponding to it". For: "Does the solipsist also say that only he can play chess?"

Philo: "– or tennis! The solipsist's, or mystic's, claimed necessarily universal Pure Self is no real embodied individual".

Nietz: "the world is not an organism at all, but chaos" – "'nature's conformity to law'...exists only thanks to your ["physicists"] interpretation ...it is...only a naïve humanitarian [later: "too human"] adjustment and distortion of meaning...because laws are absolutely *lacking*". "'Regularity' in succession is only a metaphorical expression, *as if* a rule were being followed here; not a fact". "'Things' do not behave regularly, according to a *rule*: there are no things – they are fictions invented by us". "The world...is...a fable and approximation...'in flux'...a state of becoming, as [objectively] a falsehood always changing...there is no 'truth'".

Philo: "Physics as objective cannot be interpretation. And distortion of what meaning thereby already accepted as given? Moreover, everything as always Chaotically wrong would include everything as right, which would mean no distinction, no right or wrong. That is to say, universal chaos would include universal order, thereby dissolving all distinction between chaos and order, truth and falsity, dissolving all meaning".

Nietz: "consciousness has developed only under...the need for communication...[by "signs"] of language...It was only as a social animal that man acquired self-consciousness...each of us will always succeed in becoming conscious only of what is not individual but 'average'...governed by...the perspective of the herd. Fundamentally, all our actions are altogether incomparably personal, unique, and infinitely individual; there is no doubt of that...the world of which we can become conscious is only a surface- and sign-world...relatively stupid...herd signal; all becoming conscious involves a great and thorough corruption, falsification, reduction to superficialities and generalization. Ultimately ...consciousness becomes a danger...a disease...we 'know' (or believe or imagine) just as much as may be useful in the interests of the human herd ...and...'utility' is ultimately also a mere belief, something imaginary".

Philo: "Again, you claim, mistakenly, to interpret falsity as objective, and that every person is absolutely Alone – in what you earlier described as a similar, comparable, prison world of inescapable error [see p.29] – which would be far too, impossibly self-isolating. So-called absolutely unique individuality and action always beyond language must be self-defeating, meaningless. And conscious life condemned as always disease – that would have to include 'gay science' – would join those who suffer life, as for instance Socrates finally revealed [see p.24]".

Nietz: "The intellect cannot criticize itself, simply because it cannot be compared".

Philo: "Are we not all more or less intellectually critical of intellect?"

Nietz: I mean "human intellect cannot avoid seeing itself in its own perspectives, and only in these" – "consciousness constitutes only one state of our spiritual and psychic world (perhaps a pathological state)".

Philo: "But pathological from what perspective? That which is said to be always beyond our perception is totally misleading, self-defeating. To repeat, the world so called is always relatively not Absolutely in human terms; conceptual perception is only relatively universal. And as you came to see, a 'tyrant...[of] conditions...fails to perceive...its relativity'".

Nietz: Yet still: "The art of associating with people depends essentially on an aptitude (requiring long practice) for accepting and eating a meal in whose cuisine one has no confidence".

Philo: "– all too often all too human people!"

Nietz: "words dilute and brutalize; words depersonalize; words make the uncommon common" – "to understand one another: we must...employ the same words for the same kind of internal experiences, we must in the end have experiences *in common*...the undergoing only of average and *common* experiences...One must...thwart this natural, all-too-natural... evolution of man to the similar, the ordinary, the average, the gregarious [or "herd-like"] – to the *ignoble!*"

Philo: "Communicating with one another or oneself, understanding any meaning so called, is essentially in relatively social, shareable concepts".

Nietz: "One has to get rid of the bad taste of wanting to be in agreement with many...what can be common has ever but little value". "A great man...knows he is incommunicable: he finds it tasteless to be familiar". "Every superior human being [later: "of an elevated taste"] will instinctively aspire after [and "remains hidden...in"] a secret [or "private"] citadel where he is *set free* from ["trafficking with"] the crowd ...where, as its exception, he may forget the rule [later: "of the *average* ...the commonness"] 'man' – except...[when] impelled by an even stronger instinct to...voluntarily assume this burden and displeasure ["for knowledge"]...he would...have to say...'The devil can take my good taste! the rule is more interesting...than I'...and would go *down*".

Philo: "– like 'The tragedy begins' for your wise Zarathustra? [see p.38]

But forgetting all language, ceasing to express any conceptual rule, would lose all rational meaning so called including 'good taste' or 'wisdom'. Also to communicate, to share, does not always mean to go down or under; and objectivity itself demands the devil take personal taste and instinct too!"

Nietz: Later I wrote that "the continued existence of the rule is the precondition for the value of the exception". But still: "We no longer have a sufficiently high estimate of ourselves when we communicate. Our true [or "real", *eigentlichen*] experiences...could not communicate themselves ...they lack words...The speaker has already *vulgarized* himself by speaking" – "in decay [or "degenerating"]...by...becoming mediocre" – "almost any word...would finally seem...a weakening and moderating metaphor – as too human". Or as I wrote earlier, even "every metaphor of perception is individual and without its equal...all attempts to classify it".

Witt: "Whereof one cannot speak..."? Once more, "a nothing would serve just as well as a something about which nothing could be said".

Philo (facing Nietzsche): "How could one morally estimate, or judge oneself at all without language? And how can you say or believe that truly, really or properly our experiences lack words? Truth and falsity belong directly to language: it is statements made that are true or false. Poetry, even 'nonsense poetry', is essentially composed in some rational everyday language, in conceptually defined terms; and the poetic, as well as plain language, certainly is not always vulgar or average. Fine or good taste is also often articulated. You too have spoken frequently of 'noble taste'; even claiming 'all life is dispute over taste and tasting!'".

Witt: "Every artist has been influenced by others and shows traces of that influence in his works; but his significance for us is nothing but his personality".

Nietz: "Unconsciously we seek out the principles and dogmas that are in keeping with our temperament...our character".

Witt: "It is sometimes said that a man's philosophy is a matter of temperament, and there is something in this".

Nietz: "philosophical systems...all have in them one point which is irrefutable, a personal touch...a picture of the philosopher...*personality*". "In the philosopher...there is nothing whatever impersonal; and, above all, his morality bears decided and decisive testimony to *who he is*".

Philo: "Meaning as personal is indeed nothing impersonal. A person as such is never an objective thing, yet is essentially defined, conceptually recognized as a kind of person. And again, morality is never decisive".

Nietz: "If the individual had not cared about, *his* 'truth', that is, about his being right..." – that means "the *thinker's personal struggle*".

Philo: "To repeat: understanding must distinguish between thinking, which never settles anything, and definitions as objective conceptual kinds of particular knowledge, People as rational make, in a sense create, essentially defined statements of either objective or subjective meanings".

Nietz: The philosopher expresses "prejudiced...heart's desire...in fact, the 'love of *his* wisdom'" – that is the philosopher's "spirit and taste" – also as "creative positing" – "not good taste, not bad taste, but *my* taste".

Witt: "'taste' cannot create...Taste makes things *acceptable*...a great creator has no need of taste...I have taste...taste has nothing to do with creative power. Taste is a refinement of sensitivity; but sensitivity does not do anything, it is purely receptive".

Philo: "Yes, taste makes personally acceptable, in contrast to whatever needs to be accepted for an objective purpose.

"And as indicated before [see p.26], genuine opponents are only within each different kind of practice. Strange as it may at first seem, there never are any genuine battles between scientists or philosophers as people, as personalities, for any battle in science or philosophy is nothing personal! The objective practices of science and philosophy each remain relatively completely untouched by subjectivity, even when the personal is defined, or personal prejudice attempts to hide objective realities. To speak of 'my philosophy' is, accordingly, as potentially misleading as to speak of 'my science'. The philosopher, correctly, makes some objective descriptive statements about language, while the scientist explains, makes objective empirical experiments, or deductions in principle, or provides statistics".

Witt: To repeat, "we encounter philosophical problems...when we start constructing sentences not for practical purposes"; "it is the particular use of a word only which gives the word its meaning".

Nietz: "Morality is...*practical*...'How should one act?'" – "the practical sphere, the sphere of utility" – that means "the practical interest, the personal utility of all knowledge".

Philo (directly facing Nietzsche): "Knowledge is exclusively scientific, And again too, what you say of 'the philosopher' needs to taken, in an objective sense, to mean only 'the philosopher as moral', giving moral concepts. For the practical is definitely not synonymous with the moral: distinction needs to be recognized between different senses of 'practical', as objective actions, including of will, or subjective, such as intentions.

"If I may add here, Kant took 'practical' to mean 'moral', and as a metaphysician most confusingly, mistakenly, claimed a priori knowledge of all possible 'theoretical philosophy (natural science)' and 'practical philosophy (ethical science)', as practical concerning everything 'which *ought to be*'. Once more: a priori knowledge is a figment of imagination, philosophy is never theoretical, and the practical is not only ethics. Kant's *Critique of Practical Reason* [1788] further proclaims a sole categorical imperative, an early formulation being: 'Act only according to that maxim ...you can...will as universal law'. But this imperative called 'within', in principle determining 'the will of every rational being' – trying to expand moral, also aesthetic, personal judgment about wilful actions to objective universal law – is only immoral and senseless tyrannical presumption!"

62

Nietz: An "unscientific basic tendency...[is] to interpret and inflate individual personal experiences into universal judgments" – as with "all romantic...ambiguous, inflated, oppressive art that deprives the spirit of its very severity and cheerfulness". For "to be a lawgiver is a tyranny".

Philo: "But offering relative guidance can be most useful, helpful! So please clarify your view here in more detail".

Nietz: "I do not wish to promote any morality". "I am a law only for my own [kind]". Accordingly, concerning moral rules, "first produce them out of oneself, as one should do...as conditions of precisely *our own* existence and growth, which we recognize and acknowledge independently of whether other men grow with us under similar or different conditions".

Once I expressed to a friend: "One should make one's own ideal of mankind prevail, and overpower one's fellow men as well as oneself with it – that's acting creatively!" – "This much is certain: I wish to force mankind to decisions which will determine its entire future". However: "Whatever kind of bizarre ideal one may follow...one should not demand that it be *the* ideal...One should have it in order to distinguish oneself". "Let everyone be his (or her) own true follower". For "to experience one's own judgment as a universal law...betrays that you have not...created for yourself an ideal...that could never be somebody else's".

Witt: "In what sense have you *got* what you are talking about and saying that only you have got it?...if...you exclude [the possibility of] other people's having something, it loses its sense to say that you have it ...In as much as it cannot be any one else's it is not mine either".

Nietz: "every action...[is] altogether unique and irretrievable...all regulations about actions relate only to their coarse exterior...*any* action ...remains impenetrable...We [too each]...are new, unique, incomparable". In thus: "'Consciousness'...known to ourselves alone".

Witt: "I know only indirectly what he sees, but directly what I see" embodies an absolutely misleading picture...I can't be said to know indirectly what the other has if I can't be said to know it directly".

Nietz: At the very outset of my "free thinking", in 1876, I wrote that: "The moral man...presumes that that which is essential to his heart must also be [so]...of all". Then a decade later: "the free spirit answers himself ...by generalizing his case, to decide thus about his experience: 'As it happened to me', he tells himself, 'so must it happen to everyone'".

Witt: "If I say of myself that it is only from my own case [essentially privately] that I know...must I not say the same of other people too? And how can I generalize the *one* case so irresponsibly?...Suppose everyone had a box with something in it: we call it a "beetle"...No one can look into anyone else's box, and everyone says he knows [it "only from his own case"]...Here it would be quite possible for everyone to have something different in his box...the box might even be empty".

"The essential thing about [so-called ever] private experience is really not that each person possesses his own exemplar, but that nobody knows whether other people also have *this* or something else. The assumption [of different "sensation"] would thus be possible – though unverifiable". "Always get rid of the idea of the [essentially] private object in this way: assume that it constantly changes, but that you do not notice the change".

Philo: "For that would be the far too self-orientated view of the introspective mediator or thinker, including Descartes, even the solipsist mistakenly claiming only directly to care about 'my truth', 'my world'. If all the world is my ideal, then what a wretched fool am I!"

"Against the entire unrealizably extreme introspective, meditative, even solipsistic tradition of many mystics and philosophers (in the West including Descartes, Schopenhauer, Kierkegaard and Nietzsche), it must be misleading, a conceptual blunder, to claim to externalize or generalize from only oneself; there cannot be any always purely private meaning, for the descriptive reason that there would be no way at all of distinguishing objectivity and subjectivity. It is only oppressive senseless presumption to assert categorically that personal imperative – need of one's heart – must be the same for everyone. The introspective ascetic blunders in urging first go within, follow one's own heart and 'wilfully act' before, entirely isolated from the outer world, without all else. For there cannot be any wilfulness prior to practice, or any absolutely complete Privacy Alone".

Witt: "There is no subjective sureness that I know something". "An inner experience cannot shew me that I *know* something".

Philo: "– or decisively establish, determine, define correctness or mistake".

Nietz: "the psychological derivation of the belief in things"– that shows "judgment is a belief ["a strong conviction"]...*not* knowledge!"

Witt: "a mental state of conviction...may be the same whether it is knowledge or false belief" – "complete conviction, the total absence of doubt...is *subjective* certainty. But when is something objectively certain? When a mistake is not possible".

Nietz: "The question of [moral] values is more *fundamental* than the question of certainty: the latter...presupposing...[the former] has already been answered".

Witt: "What I know, I believe". But: "What is a telling ground for something is not anything *I* decide" – "it needs to be *objectively* established that I am not making a mistake". "'I know that' means 'I am incapable of being wrong about that'. But where I am so must admit of being established objectively". "One always forgets the expression 'I thought I knew'".

Philo: "Saying 'I know' never guarantees that knowledge – excepting everything which is required to have illustrative knowledge for use of the concepts 'I' and 'know'".

Witt: One must avoid "the elementary mistake of confusing one's thoughts [or feelings] with one's knowledge".

Philo: "– elementary yet all too common. Again, three very different kinds of understanding are thought, knowledge and conceptual sense".

Witt: "If 'I know etc.' is conceived as a grammatical proposition, of course the 'I' cannot be important. And it properly means 'There is no such thing as doubt in this case' or 'The expression 'I do not know' makes no sense in this case'. And of course it follows from this that 'I *know*' makes no sense either".

Philo: "In objective practice, as in science or philosophy, the personal must be put aside relatively entirely".

Witt: As just said, "a telling ground...is not anything *I* decide". "There is therefore no occult act of *naming* an object that in itself can give a word a meaning...There is a name only where there is a technique of using it...There is no essentially private [objective] justification for I couldn't know whether anything that is essentially private *is a justification*" – "justification consists in appealing to something independent" – and "'sensation' is a word of our common language, not of one intelligible to me alone. So the use of this word stands in need of a justification which everybody understands". "An 'inner process' stands in need of outward criteria".

Nietz: Once more, there is "no *criterion of truth* [in itself], but an *imperative* [of morality] concerning that which *should* count as true".

Witt: "What is the criterion for meaning something different? Not only what he [one] takes as evidence for it, but also how he [one feels and] reacts". There really is "characteristic expression of pain, of fear, of joy".

"it is sensible to ask 'How do you know?', and criteria can be given which cannot be given in one's own case. In one's own case it makes no sense to ask 'How do I know?'" – "'I know where I am feeling pain', 'I know that I feel it here' is as wrong as 'I know that I am in pain'. But 'I know where you touched my arm' is right".

Philo: "No one can have another's – or know their own – thoughts or feelings; sentiment is never objective. And no criterion is Absolute. Yet any meaning is defined objectively by means of public actions".

Nietz: "nothing is 'given' as real except our world of desires and passions...of our drives [or "impulses"] – for thinking is only the ['given' essential] relationship of these drives to one another".

Witt: "There is always the danger of wanting to find an expression's meaning by contemplating the expression itself, and the frame of mind in which one uses it ["in the feeling it gives one"], instead of always thinking of [recognizing] the practice".

Philo: "Again, to start with the will to power, claimed as the most fundamental condition, or impulse, must really involve bodily actions, behaviour, as conceptually so called with objective certainty".

Nietz: "the *erroneousness* of the world...is the surest and firmest thing ...we find proof after proof thereof...Is it not enough to suppose grades [or "degrees"] of apparentness...? Why could the world *which is of any concern to us* – not be a fiction?"

Philo: "All proof, correctness or error is objective. Objective reality needs to be accepted as unjustifiable, for the descriptive reason that every proof is an objective procedure and nothing can justify itself".

Witt (facing Nietzsche): "I need a criterion of identity for the sensation; and then the possibility of error also exists". You might also say to me: "'Are you not really a behaviourist in disguise? Aren't you at bottom really saying that everything except human behaviour is a fiction?' – If I do speak of a fiction, then it is of a *grammatical* fiction". "What we deny is that the picture of the inner process gives us the correct idea of the use". "Introspection can never lead to a definition. It can only lead to a psychological statement about the introspector".

"If intuition [or instinct] is an inner voice – how do I know *how* I am to obey it? And how do I know that it doesn't mislead me? For if it can guide me right, it can also guide me wrong". To repeat: "A definition surely serves to establish the meaning of a sign...in the present case [of introspection, when "I concentrate...inwardly"] I have no criterion of correctness...here we can't talk about 'right'".

Nietz: I must again confess "my feeling of *isolation*. Neither among the living nor among the dead is there anyone with whom I feel any kinship. This...experience I've had, ever since I was a child, of living with this growing isolation". "I'm still just as alone as I was in my childhood".

Witt: While writing the *Tractatus* I noted too "the way I have travelled: Idealism singles men out from the world as unique, solipsism singles me alone out, and at last I see that I too belong with the rest of the world".

Philo: "If nothing beyond oneself were admitted, how could any other individual, 'we' or 'I' be admitted? We understand one another talking of personal meanings because every linguistic expression is communicable, shareable, socially defined through public actions with objective certainty, allowing any participant to recognize who or what is stated".

Witt: Once again: "In as much as it [anything claimed] cannot be any one else's it is not mine either". "Don't concern yourself with what, presumably, no one but you grasps!" – "The [unshareable] 'private experience' is a degenerate construction of our grammar...[a] grammatical monster...In what sense is a thought of mine secret? If I think aloud it can be heard" – "we only say that someone speaks to himself if, in the ordinary sense of the words, he *can speak* ["an audible language"]".

Philo: "Any language is essentially some, more or less, social activity. Our language shows that no one is ever absolutely completely Alone".

Witt: "Consciousness is as clear in his [another's] face and behaviour, as in myself".

Objective Practice
and Subjective Interpretation

Witt: "In order to describe the phenomenon of language, one must describe a practice". "The use of the word *in practice* is its meaning".

Nietz: "'to know'...[is] to impose upon chaos as much regularity and form as our practical needs require" – which again means "the practical interest, the personal utility of all knowledge".

Witt: "Practice gives the words their sense".

Philo: "One must distinguish between objective concepts or knowledge and personal moral evaluations, of single of group subjectivity, expressed in objective acts of freewill".

Nietz: "There exists neither a natural right nor a natural wrong". "Rights can in the first instance be traced back to *tradition*, tradition to some *agreement*".

Witt\; "to communicate, people must agree with one another about the meanings of words". "If language is to be a means of communication there must be agreement not only in definitions but also (queer as this may sound) in judgments".

Philo: "And 'judgment' is roughly synonymous with 'belief'".

Nietz: "That a great deal of *belief* must be present...that doubt concerning all essential values is *lacking* – that is the precondition of every living thing...something must be held to be true – *not* that something *is* true".

Witt: "a great deal of stage-setting in the language is presupposed if the mere act of naming is to make sense...what is presupposed is the existence of the grammar".

Nietz: "Believing is the primal beginning even in every sense impression". Furthermore, "only in connection and relation of many judgments is there any surety".

Witt: "learning is based on believing" – "we are taught *judgments* and their connexion with other judgments. *A totality* of judgments is made plausible to us. When we first begin to *believe* anything, what we believe is not a single proposition, it is a whole system of propositions. (Light dawns gradually over the whole.)"

"agreement decides what [statement] is true and what is false...human beings...agree in the *language* they use. That is not agreement in opinions but in form of life".

Nietz: "This tree...if it wished to speak, it would find no one who understood it".

Witt: "If a lion could talk, we could not understand him".

"A symbol cannot by itself be a symbol; what makes it a symbol is belonging to a system of symbols...a grammatical system". "A word only has meaning in a grammatical system...[as] used". To repeat: "the grammar of our ordinary language...is already there"; for it is "the herd which has created this language".

Nietz: Again too: "'It is given' – that is also a doctrine of submission". "What is needed above all is an absolute scepticism toward all inherited concepts".

Witt: "judgment...must begin with not-doubting".

Philo: "It must make sense to be able to doubt, deny, conceive as false, any statement of contingent fact".

Witt: – "a principle of speaking for and against". But: "If you are not certain of any fact, you cannot be certain of the meaning of your words either". "A doubt that doubted everything would not be a doubt".

Nietz: "it ["meaning"] is not a fact...only interpretation".

Witt: "one is not playing the game, or is playing it wrong, if one does not recognize objects with certainty". "Doubt comes *after* belief" – for "doubting itself presupposes certainty" – "we must commit ourselves to the use of the words".

Philo: "One cannot genuinely doubt commitment to some objective certainty of the definitions used in making any statement, any correctness or mistake, or any doubt. And that also means any objective language, expressing its relatively essential repeatable meanings, is independent of any particular individual's commitment".

Witt: Once more: "We must distinguish between a necessity in the system and a necessity of the system as a whole". "If I use a symbol I must be committing myself...and...I am committed to a future usage" – as "guided" or "led by language". "What is essential is that in using the word I commit myself to a rule of use" – "there must be rules, for language must be systematic...if there are no rules there is no game" – "what makes it ["grammar"] not arbitrary is its use".

Nietz: "Trust in reason...proves only...usefulness for life, proved by experience". "What 'useful' means is entirely dependent upon the *intention*".

Witt: Use as "'measuring' is partly determined by a certain constancy in the results of measurement" – even "the result is part of the technique".

Philo: "– that means technique is only to some extent, in some sense, justified by agreement in the same action, in obtaining the same results.

"Rational language does not prohibit its use even when a person denies commitment to its essential conceptual rules. People also act with inner motive, or personal need. Non-causal intention is involved in subjective moral evaluations, which enhance or slander – but can never determine – objective causal actions. For willing is always bodily acting more or less consciously chosen as intentional, purposeful, goal-orientated behaviour".

Nietz: Different people "with different intentions and modes of interpretation could read out of the same 'Nature', and with regard to the same phenomena" different meanings – "'reality' is always only simplification for practical ends, or [objectively] a deception through the coarseness of organs" – "'knowing' intellect encounters a coarse [or "crude"], already-created world, fabricated".

Witt: "it is easy to get into that dead-end in philosophy, where one believes that the difficulty of the task consists in our having to describe phenomena that are hard to get hold of...Where we find ordinary language too crude, and it looks as if we were having to do, not with the phenomena of every-day".

Nietz: Concerning "the [scientist's] mechanistic interpretation of the world...description and not explanation is all that is possible".

Witt: "It was true to say that our ["philosophical"] considerations could not be scientific ones...We must do away with all *explanation*, and description alone must take its place". "Our method is *purely descriptive*; the descriptions we give are not hints of explanations".

Philo: "Also once more, science as objective is never interpretation".

Nietz: "'Interpretation', the introduction of [subjective] meaning – [is] not 'explanation'...There are no facts, everything is in flux, incomprehensible, elusive; what is relatively most enduring is – our opinions [or "judgments"]" – "everything of which we become conscious is...interpreted...We never encounter 'facts'...both the deed and the doer are fictions" – "there is...only interpretations. We cannot establish any fact 'in itself'..."Everything is subjective", you say; but even this is interpretation. The 'subject' ["an interpreter"] is not something given, it is something added and invented and projected...the world is knowable; but it is *interpretable* otherwise, it has...countless meanings...It is our needs that interpret the world; our drives and their For and Against. Every drive is a kind of lust to rule; each one has its perspective".

Witt: Again, "a principle of speaking for and against".

Nietz: Yet still: "Necessity is not a fact but an interpretation".

Philo: To repeat, necessity must distinguish its relatively completely different conceptual senses: either objective conceptual necessity, which is never contingent fact, or moral necessity which is always personal interpretation".

Nietz: Some five years into "my 'free thinking'" [since HH in 1876], I continued to maintain: "truths...they still appear to us too much like 'winged dreams'...as though we could awaken from these truths of ours!" – "Granted this too is only interpretation – and you will be eager enough to raise this objection? – well, so much the better".

Philo: "But here, one more time, the question arises: how could every meaning be merely interpretation of dream? For if all were interpretation, then that would have to include this very view. The dream world as such is always personal meaning, never itself objective (although objectively defined), never correct or mistaken – and only recognized as such after awakening, that is, as subsequently compared to waking reality".

Witt: And again, "if I am dreaming...it is also being dreamed that these words have any meaning".

Philo: "Any rule could be given any, more or less practical, sense. Whereof it is said one can never speak, one may simply reply: "But I do". There are myriad possible interpretations of all rules or symbols. Who or what says how to apply a picture, or how to use a symbol?"

Witt: "a symbol – which can be reinterpreted in any way whatsoever". "'Whatever I do is, on some interpretation, in accord with the [any] rule' – That is not what we ought to say, but rather: any interpretation still hangs in the air along with what it interprets, and cannot give it any support. Interpretations by themselves do not determine meaning".

Nietz: "supposing that a philosopher has always been first of all a hermit...he will doubt whether a philosopher *could* have 'final and real' opinions at all; whether behind each of his caves there does not and must not lie, another, deeper cave – a stranger, more comprehensive world beyond the surface, an abyss behind every ground, beneath every 'foundation'. Every philosophy is a foreground philosophy...there is something arbitrary [and "suspicious"] in the fact...that he stopped digging and laid his spade aside *here*...Every philosophy also *conceals* a philosophy; every opinion is also a hiding-place, every word also a mask".

Witt: 'If I have exhausted the justifications ["for my following the rule"] I have reach bedrock, and my spade is turned. Then I am inclined to say: 'This is simply what I do'" – "my reasons will soon give out. And then I shall act [surely], without reasons".

"This was our paradox: no course of action could be determined by a rule, because every course of action can be made out to accord with the rule. The answer was: if everything can be made out to accord with the rule, then it can also be made out to conflict with it. And so there would be neither accord nor conflict here. It can be seen that there is a misunderstanding here from the mere fact that in the course of our argument we give one interpretation after another; as if each one contented us at least for a moment, until we thought of yet another standing behind it. What this shows is that there is a way of grasping a rule which is *not* an *interpretation*, but which is exhibited in what we call "obeying the rule" and "going against it" in actual cases. Hence there is an inclination to say: every action according to the rule is an interpretation. But we ought to restrict the term 'interpretation' to the substitution of one expression of the rule for another. And hence also, 'obeying a rule' is a practice. And to *think* one is obeying a rule is not to obey a rule. Hence it is not possible to obey a rule 'privately': otherwise thinking one was obeying a rule would be the same thing as obeying it".

Philo: "From this key highly insightful descriptive argument just given, I see first the sceptic argues that every action can be interpreted to follow any rule, therefore there can be no rule-determined action. But the correct answer is that if every action admits any interpretation as rule-following, then it also admits the opposing interpretation, and every action able both to follow and go against any rule makes it self-contradictory to speak of obeying or disobeying. This latter argument is descriptive, not refutation, nor justification. Philosophy also is never opinion. Describing conceptual rule-following is never 'private', interpretation or thinking as such, but public practice. Thinking of rule-following never is rule-following itself. Action is never interpreted as rule-following; interpretations never define, determine correctness or mistake, but are always subjective, personal, with all their terms objectively defined. Potentially infinite regression of thought interpretations shows our already accepting that conceptual rules are understood with objective certainty in practice".

Nietz: "To submit, to follow, openly or in secret..." – "all becoming conscious involves a great and thorough corruption, falsification, reduction to superficialities and generalization". Also again: "'Regularity' in succession is only...*as if* a rule were being followed".

Philo (facing Nietzsche): "Yet as you have recognized previously, 'the commander...must...practice obedience even in commanding'".

Nietz: "that you take this or that judgment...to be right – may [mean you] simply have accepted blindly".

Witt: "When I obey a rule, I do not choose. I obey the rule *blindly*".

Nietz: To repeat: "Rights can in the first instance be traced back to *tradition*, tradition to some *agreement*".

Witt: "One does not learn to obey a rule by first learning the use of the word 'agreement'. Rather, one learns the meaning of 'agreement' by learning to follow a rule. If you want to understand what it means 'to follow a rule', you have already to be able to follow a rule...I don't make use of agreement of human beings to affirm identity. 'What criterion do you use, then?' None at all". "What I do [in "the beginning"] is not...to identify my sensation by criteria: but to repeat an expression". "To use a word without a justification does not mean to use it without right".

Philo: "I can wilfully choose to join in a practice or not. Yet obeying a rule is more or less conscious and practical, that is, an impersonal act of objectively certain agreement itself without feeling, thought or question".

Witt: "A rule is best described as being like a garden path in which you are trained to walk, and which is convenient...You are not compelled to do so, but you just do it".

Nietz: In the higher men, "the spirit is...as much at home in the senses as the senses are at home in the spirit". "We want to hold fast to our senses and to our faith in them – and think their consequences through to the end!...and not criticize it [the "world"] away as false!"

Witt: Once more, "it has no meaning to say that a game has always been played wrong".

Philo: "The world, of objective practice and subjectivity, cannot be only illusion. What in time can't be factually true or correct can't be factually false or mistaken, and vice-versa".

Nietz: "the *sense for facts*, [is] the last developed and most valuable of all the senses". Now "our attitude toward art [is]: we do not demand beautiful illusory lies from it, etc.; brutal positivism reigns, recognizing facts". "One should not conceal and corrupt the facts of how our thoughts have come to us". "Error is *cowardice* – every achievement of knowledge is a consequence of courage, of severity toward oneself, of cleanliness toward oneself".

Witt: Again: "Courage is always original" and "who does not lie is already original enough".

Philo (facing Nietzsche): "And it has to be said that overcoming the falsity of metaphysics must include your claimed 'Scientific philosophy' of 'cleansing knowledge', of always created, 'imported' facts as thought, interpreted!"

Nietz: I indeed still held that "a 'free spirit'...cares nothing for what is fixed...the whole of nature...[is] merely...a metaphor".

Philo: "One must also have enough courage and honesty to recognize that – your inspirational morality as personal aside (which also needs to be acknowledged as objectively defined) – all you say, Nietzsche, of real objectivity relatively totally in itself as merely 'the cult of 'objectivity'' is entirely wrong, mistaken and immoral. You use such terms as 'objectivity', 'knowledge', 'concept', 'fact', 'act', 'use', 'correct' or 'mistaken', never as given in everyday practice, but always 'found' as imaginative creation of coarse, deceptive, lying personal moral belief, interpretation, perspective. And you say the philosopher's ''knowing' is *creating*', but the philosopher never knows as such. What's more, all objectivity, correctness or error, is mistakenly claimed as in the context of subjective psychology".

Witt: It is necessary that "we make a radical break with the idea that language...always serves the same purpose: to convey thoughts".

Philo (facing Nietzsche): "You declare 'we do not permit ourselves any bridges-of-lies to ancient Ideals...for ever 'bringing us down''. Yet you lament being 'Only a poet!...That must lie...on deceptive word-bridges' [see p.48]. Crucially, you denounce ascetics: to 'reduce the physical world to an illusion...nothing but errors!...to deny...'reality'...a cruel violation of *reason*'. So too you reject Absolute Morality of '*hostility to life*...slander... a 'will to decline'...[which affirms] life *must* constantly and inevitably be in the wrong'. Such words, as unpoetic, express moral and objective right criticism of condemning this life as false, all the world as error or illusion. Your wilful thought of all conceptual communication as 'interpretation' is thus extremely poor, 'degenerated' [see p.54], error hostile to rational life!

"Likewise, when you wrote of idealists proclaiming that 'the [every-day] requirements of the individual...are to be regarded as some thing contemptible or a matter of indifference'; and you added that 'we too have inherited something of this poison of contempt for what is closest'. It has to be said, to indeed a far greater extent, that your invented and believed Chaos, which one may call your "other world of primal and ongoing Chaos" as 'incomprehensible, elusive' [see p.69] – completely void of all definiteness, spaceless and timeless, neither being nor even becoming – is a senseless blunder of prejudice, denying, condemning everyday linguistic reality. The concepts of 'Chaos', 'Void' and 'Nothing' are only most extreme unrealizable abstract Ideals of claimed universal necessity. To repeat, Nature as so called is never absolutely completely Valueless, Emptiness or Nothingness, but always defined relatively in itself as some actual, factual kind of objectivity.

"Your view of nothing but interpretation, wilful thought interpretation, is dark and gloomy, too self-isolating, self-oppressing: as you earlier have said of others, suffering life, 'you yourself' vengefully 'destroy your own judgment!'. It must be wrong, both mistaken and immoral, self-mockingly to turn reason against itself, claiming it needs to recognize that reality, or any world, remains always beyond its grasp – of mere thought".

Nietz: Previously, I have maintained that "between two utterly different spheres, as between subject and object, there is...at the utmost an...artistic formation of metaphors". "Actions are never what they appear to us to be! ...all actions are essentially unknown" – "every action...[is] altogether unique...We [too each]...are...unique, incomparable".

Philo: "As if real actions in social practice, wrongly devalued by you, were insufficient to determine shared real meaning! You also said each of us can become 'conscious only of what is not individual but...herd signal' [see p.59]. But even that essentially means no individual, person or thing, can ever be Absolutely Uniquely Alone, or Higher, that is, without all the linguistic world. And judging decisive meaning, or definition, as merely strong interpretative thought would mean no difference in kind between them, abolishing distinction between objectivity and subjectivity. How to tell any falsity, illusion, error or doubt if not always through some defined genuine truth, reality, correctness or certainty? – That must be accepted as relatively fixed in unpoetic, uninterpreted, unthought, objective practice.

"Truth or reality distinguishes relatively completely different senses as objective, impersonal, public or subjective, personal, private. These two kinds of perception, even objective and subjective 'worlds', are entirely mutually exclusive; yet also necessarily relate as the developing world – which requires each embodied person's commitment in practice, more or less consciously acknowledged. Every meaning is objectively defined, as conceptual kind of known individual, so called, recognized by someone".

Having spoken these words, Philo became silent.

Language-games

Witt: "I used to believe that there was the everyday language that we all usually spoke and a primary language that expressed what we really knew...[However] our everyday language already is the language". "It is *primarily* the apparatus of our ordinary language, of our word-language, that we call language, and then other things by analogy or comparability with this". We need "to have a clear view...of what the ideal [or "model"] is, namely an object of comparison...instead of making a prejudice of it to which everything has to conform" – "a preconceived idea ["of crystalline purity"] to which reality *must* correspond".

Nietz: For, once more, "to be a lawgiver is a tyranny" – with the too idealistic or ascetic person making "oppressing...excessive claims and afterwards idolizing this tyrann[y]".

Witt: "The first step is the one that altogether escapes notice. We talk of processes and states and leave their ["yet uncomprehended...yet unexplored"] nature undecided. Sometime perhaps we shall know more about them – we think. But that is just what commits us to a particular way of looking at the matter".

Nietz: "that master expedient of representing everything as having already been discovered, with nothing still on the way and as yet uncertain".

Witt: "We see that what we call "sentence" and "language" has not the formal unity that I imagined, but is the family of structures more or less related to one another". As mentioned before: "At the root of all this there was a false and idealized picture of the use of language...But...instead we must describe...related language games" – "these [linguistic] phenomena have no one thing [essence] in common...but...are *related* to one another in many different ways...I will try to explain [or rather describe] this".

Philo: "Each and every rational language practice or game is certainly a rule-governed activity".

Witt: "We shall compare the use of language to playing a game according to exact rules, because all philosophical troubles arise from making up too simple a system of rules".

Nietz: Again: "What strange simplification and falsification mankind lives in!" Moreover, "science itself *requires* justification (which is not to say that such justification exists)".

Witt: As said earlier [on p.71], "one learns the meaning of 'agreement' by learning to follow a rule". And "for an explanation...We must know what explanation means". Similarly philosophical (like aesthetic) reasons are essentially "further descriptions".

Philo: "Philosophy is never science, justification, knowledge or proof. There never is any objective justifying argument for objective linguistic practice; once more for the descriptive reason that any justification is essentially defined as objective practice, and nothing can justify itself. There cannot be any objective justification for any concepts as such, as essentially objective.

(facing Wittgenstein) "Please elaborate on this appealing to one's sense of unjustifiable objectivity".

Witt: "Nothing we do can be defended definitively [or "absolutely and finally"]. But only by reference to something else that is established [or "not questioned"]. I.e. no reason can be given why you should act (or should have acted) like this, except that by doing so you bring about such and such a situation, which again you have to accept as an aim". "In certain circumstances, for example, we regard a calculation as sufficiently checked. What gives us a right to do so? Experience? May that not have deceived us? Somewhere we must be finished with justification, and then there remains the proposition that *this* is how we calculate".

"a language-game is only possible if one trusts something" – and that means objectively – "we have to...*accept* the everyday language-game, and to note *false* accounts of the matter *as* false. The primitive language-game which children are taught needs no justification; [here] attempts at justification need to be rejected".

The beginning as well as "the end [of "giving grounds"] is not an ungrounded presupposition: it is an ungrounded way of acting". "Giving grounds...justifying the evidence, comes to an end; – but the end is not certain propositions striking us immediately as true, i.e. it is not a kind of seeing on our part; it is our *acting*, which lies at the bottom of the language-game". "Sure evidence is what we *accept* as sure...[for] acting". "To know its [a word's] meaning is to use it in the same way as other people do...determined by a consensus of action...not a consensus of opinion. We all act the same way".

Philo: "Objective not subjective agreement".

Witt: "in philosophical investigation: the difficulty...here is: to stop".

Philo: "That means to recognize every concept as description: to stop expecting and trying to get beyond description, in philosophy, by asking totally misleadingly for scientific justification, explanation or opinion".

Witt: "Words are also deeds" – "and [we] write with confidence 'In the beginning was the deed'". "Is our confidence justified? What people accept as a justification – is shewn by how they think and live".

Nietz: "if ever I have laughed with the laugh of the creative lightning, which the thunder of the deed, grumbling but obedient, follows" – thus sang my Zarathustra. For again: "Believing is the primal beginning".

Philo: "In the beginning was belief? Never alone! Belief or judgment itself, thought or feeling as such, never defines anything".

"The genuine philosophical task or battle, entirely within philosophy, is to articulate concepts sufficiently in social practice, that is, different relatively essential kinds of objective meanings, distinguishing sense or senselessness of any linguistic expression. In this descriptive way, philosophy connects all languages, all meanings rationally so called".

Nietz: "philosophers...traverse the whole range of human values...and make it clear".

Witt: To repeat, "the task of philosophy is...to clarify the use of our language".

"How hard I find it to see what is right in front of my eyes!" – "one... becomes aware of the most essential when one suddenly loses it...it is so essential, therefore so ordinary". "The solution of philosophical problems can be compared with a gift in a fairy tale: in the magic castle it appears enchanted and if you look at it outside in daylight it is nothing but an ordinary bit of iron (or something of the sort)" – "philosophical...answers will only be correct if they are plain and everyday. Provided you look at them in the right [or "proper", *richtigen*] spirit, that won't matter".

Nietz: But again, "idealists of every description...hammer [out that] ...the requirements of the individual...within...the [every] day, are to be regarded as some thing contemptible or a matter of indifference".

Witt: "Now what makes it difficult...is our craving for generality...the contemptuous attitude towards the particular case". "Not only rules, but also examples are needed for establishing a practice. Our rules leave loop-holes open". "The words 'non-sense' and 'sense' get their meaning only in [with reference of] particular cases...We...talk...without giving a clear [absolutely strict] meaning to 'sense'...there is no such thing as a completed grammar" – sense is "without a *fixed* meaning".

Philo: "Our ordinary use of language is dynamic, allowing for new examples, without universally necessary meaning fixed for all time".

Witt: "what I call 'language games' (synonymous with 'primitive languages' for the most part)..." – "these games are complete; nothing is lacking...I have wanted to show by means of language-games the vague way in which we use 'language', 'proposition', 'sentence'".

Philo: "– the relatively both vague, incomplete and essential, complete use of conceptual practices, illustrated by simpler, even childlike, games".

Witt: "I have explained [or rather described]...a proposition only by giving examples". "I am giving grammatical examples". "Propositions do not all have something in common, but are a family of things having overlapping likeness...The examples give a clear enough idea".

"Now I think of the meanings as like fibres of a rope". "A rope...is not of *one* piece but consists of many interwoven, partially overlapping short strands" – "a rope...consists of fibres, but it does not get its strength from any fibre which runs through it from one end to the other, but from...a vast number of fibres overlapping".

"We are inclined to think that there must be something in common to all games, say, and that this common property is the justification for applying the general term 'game' to the various games; whereas games form a *family* the members of which have family likenesses...and these likenesses overlap". "Consider for example the proceedings that we call 'games'. I mean board-games, card games, ball games, Olympic games, and so on...you will not see something [one essence] that is common to *all*, but similarities, relationships, and...difference...we see a complicated network of similarities overlapping and criss-crossing...I can think of no better expression to characterize these similarities than "family resemblances"...between members of a family: 'games' form a family".

Nietz: Philosophers' "thinking is...a remembering, a return and a home-coming to a far-off, ancient common-household of the soul... The wonderful family resemblance of all Indian, Greek, and German philosophizing...In fact, where there is affinity of language, owing to the common philosophy of grammar".

Philo: "From what has been said on particular language-games, that is, conceptual practices, it is clear enough that some distinction is necessary between relatively completely different general kinds of such practices. For instance: the poet, moralist, lawyer, religious believer, scientist and philosopher never can contradict one another – never opponents as such, they are essentially complementary. Here genuine battles are only within each general kind of rule-governed practice. And likewise, distinction is necessary between that which is public or personal. Accordingly, there never can be any genuine battle between philosophy and science; or any genuine personal battle between philosophers, or between scientists, who as individuals express these, relatively entirely different, two main kinds of objective rational practice".

Religious Language

Philo: "And so we come to religious kind of language practice, and its relatively complete difference to not only our everyday language, but also especially to scientific language".

Nietz: "The madman...cried incessantly: 'I seek God!'...[to which the unbelievers then "laughed"] 'We have killed him...God is dead'". My "Zarathustra...is merely an old atheist". "Zarathustra the Godless!" – "this God which I created was human work and human madness, like all gods!" – "All gods are dead".

Witt: "Religion as madness is a madness springing from irreligiousness (*Irreligiosität*)".

Nietz: "religions are affairs of the rabble" – "there is no God". "God... belongs to the realm of fable".

"God is dead; but...we still have to vanquish his shadow, too". "Let us beware of thinking that the world is a living being...[it has] no purposes... When will all these [metaphysical] shadows of God cease to darken our minds? When will we complete our de-deification of nature? When may we begin to '*naturalize*' humanity...?"

"we who are godless" – we "do not permit [ourselves] any ultimate [or "final", *letzten*] Wisdom...Goodness...Power...Peace" – "we do not permit ourselves any bridges-of-lies to ancient Ideals...we are hostile from the heart to...Idealism...for ever 'drawing us upward' and precisely thereby for ever 'bringing us down'...we immoralists, we godless men of today". The "higher...man...is looking down on it ["religion"], as on a chain...so that he may not rise too high".

Philo: "Here I should at least give the reminder that every genuine judgment of correctness, error or lie is objective, not interpretation".

Nietz: "we find that which has been reverenced as God not 'godlike' but pitiable, absurd, harmful, not merely an error but *a crime against life*" – "*lies* from the bad instincts of sick, in the profoundest sense injurious natures – all the concepts 'God', 'soul', ['spirit', 'free will'] 'virtue', 'sin', 'the Beyond', 'truth', 'eternal life'...because the most injurious men ["who take revenge on life"] have been taken for great men".

"religions [are] for *sufferers* [later: "for the preservation of all the sick and suffering"]...those who suffer from life as from a disease, and they would fain treat every other experience of life as [objectively] false and impossible...[holding] hatred of the earth".

Witt: "People are religious to the extent that they believe themselves not so much *imperfect* as *sick*. Anyone who is half-way decent will think himself utterly imperfect, but the religious person thinks himself *wretched...*The Christian [or any] religion is only for the one who needs infinite help...refuge in this *ultimate* distress".

Philo: "Also, once more, conscious life condemned as always a disease joins those who suffer life, like Socrates finally revealed [see p.24]".

Nietzsche: Further, "a divinity that sacrifices itself was the strongest and most effective symbol...for...self-denial" – "those who suffer from the impoverishment of life...seek...redemption from themselves" – "lack of personality...weakened...personality that denies itself is no longer fit for anything good...'Selflessness' has no value either in heaven or on earth" – "what? is love supposed to be something unegoistic?" – "One has to be set firmly upon *oneself*...otherwise one *cannot* love at all".

Witt: Again: "Man's greatest happiness is love".

Nietz: "The priest knows only *one* great danger: that is science...The concept of ["sin",] guilt and punishment, the entire 'moral world-order', was invented *in opposition to* science...Man...shall suffer in such a way that he has need of the priest at all times. – Away with physicians!...*then one has committed the greatest crime against humanity*...to make science, culture, every kind of elevation and nobility of man impossible; the priest *rules* through the invention of sin" – "the whole religio-moral interpretation is only a form of submission to evil".

"the triumph of scientific atheism...The ungodliness of existence... atheism is simply the presupposition...that...forbids itself the lie in faith in God" – "the lie of belief in God".

Philo: "Illusory opposing danger, overrule and counter-triumph! Nature relatively in itself is impersonal objectivity. And it is a totally misleading presumption to try to use science to banish – the objectively falsely called 'lie' of – any personal faith. There never is a genuine opposition between essentially personal religion, or morality, and impersonal science".

Nietz: "The ungodliness of existence was for him ["Schopenhauer", for instance,] something given...a moral world order and ultimate moral purposes...for the sake of the salvation of the soul...has man's ["good"] conscience against it, that is considered indecent and dishonest [also "weakness, and cowardice"] by every more refined conscience".

Witt: "Schopenhauer is quite a crude mind...though he has refinement, this suddenly becomes exhausted at a certain level...Where real depth starts, his comes to an end...he never searches his conscience".

Nietz: "'The father' in God is thoroughly refuted; likewise 'the judge'".

Witt: "If the question arises as to the existence of a god or God, it plays an entirely different role to that of the existence of any person or object I ever heard of".

Nietz: "'Faith' means not *wanting* to know what is true". Moreover: "What thinking person still needs the hypothesis of a god?"

Witt: For "religious belief...different words are used: 'dogma', 'faith'. We don't talk about hypothesis, or about high probability. Nor about knowing [nor "opinion"]". "My attitude towards him ["a friend"] is an attitude towards a soul. I am not of the *opinion* that he has a soul".

Philo: "And naturally it must not be forgotten that each rational person is not only genuinely free-thinking but also passionate".

Witt: "In a religious discourse we use such expressions" – as "belief", "experience" and "evidence" – "entirely differently" in comparison to "ordinary" or "scientific" language. "The point is that if there were [scientific] evidence, this would...destroy the whole business [of religious belief]".

Philo: "Theists and atheists often mistake religious faith as scientific theory. Belief as personal never is science. It is honest, conceptually correct, to admit that existence or non-existence of divinity is never known. Theism, polytheism or atheism is always valid as belief not claiming objectivity, but invalid claiming knowledge, even absolutely complete Knowledge or Omniscience. Any claim to knowledge for or against God must be pseudo-science, pseudo-religion".

Witt: Also, to repeat: "Religious faith and superstition are quite [or "entirely", *ganz*] different. One of them results from fear and is a sort of false science. The other is a [personal] trusting".

Philo: "Any sincere religious belief is a personal affair of the heart".

Nietz: "Convictions are more dangerous enemies of truth than lies". What "has made history so violent...is the struggle [or "conflict"] of convictions...arrogant presumptuousness" – "intense feeling, which guarantees nothing at all about knowledge...[for] belief proves [or "demonstrates"] only its own strength, not the truth of what is believed" – "what first led to the [religious then metaphysical] positing of 'another world' ["behind, below, above"] in primeval times was not some impulse or need but *error* in the interpretation of certain natural events, a failure of the intellect". "Conviction is the belief that...one possesses absolute [or "unconditional"] Truth (*unbedingten Wahrheit*)...The countless people who sacrificed themselves for their convictions [of Truth]...All of them were wrong".

Philo: "May I interpose, once more, 'right' and 'wrong' can mean judgment as subjective or objective. Here I take you to mean, as made clear repeatedly before, claiming that which is now 'known' to be falsity, error. But that never means interpretation as such".

Witt: A man's personal need to pray "is just what he does in such a situation. There can be no talk of 'wrong' here...How could one say of him who must wring his hands and beseech, that he is mistaken or in an illusion". "Call it [kneeling in prayer] a sickness! What have you said by that? Nothing".

Philo: "– nothing of the heart".

Witt: "I can't contradict that person [religious believer]".

Philo: "Nothing personal can objectively contradict or be contradicted".

Witt: "you can call it [religious belief] believing the opposite, but it is entirely different from what we would normally call believing the opposite" – "this [religious] belief does not rest on the fact on which our ordinary everyday beliefs normally do rest".

"In religion talking is not metaphorical either; for otherwise it would have to be possible to say the same things in prose". Again, religious "expressions...are not similes, of course. For what can be said by way of a simile, that can also be [more or less] said without a simile".

Philo: "Relativity objectively rules all conceptual practice! The concept 'Absolute', 'Unconditional' or 'One' essentially means 'Other' than all relativity; or in other words, is only defined in relative terms as universal completeness which is indefinable, unknowable, invalidity, impossibility, absurdity, senseless – including nonsensical self-defeating paradox".

Witt: "this [pointing out contradictions] proves nothing for or against the Absolute...[one] should not argue for or against the Absolute".

Niet: "the worst of all tastes, [is] the taste for the Unconditional" – "everything Unconditional belongs in pathology".

Witt: "I wouldn't call them ["rebuke" all religious people as] unreasonable...they are certainly not *reasonable*...they don't [all] treat this as a matter of reasonability...What seems to me ludicrous...is...making it appear to be *reasonable*...[This latter is] unreasonable...superstition... cheating [oneself]".

Philo: "– only ridiculing religious belief which pretends, completely misleadingly, that it is reasonable".

Nietz: Saying "'I believe because it is absurd'" is "a banner of extreme fanaticism".

Witt: "Don't for heaven's sake, be afraid of talking nonsense! But you must pay attention to your nonsense".

Philo: "Senseless language means illegitimacy, mistake, only as some conceptual objectivity".

Witt: In religion it "does not matter at all if the words used are true or false or nonsense". For in religion "the words you utter...are not what matters [or "is important"], so much as the difference they make ...in your life". Once more, a man's religious "unshakeable belief...will show, not by reasoning or by appeal to ordinary grounds for belief, but rather by regulating for all in his life".

Philo (facing Wittgenstein): "You indicated earlier that, from winter 1914, you read Nietzsche's volume including *Twilight of the Idols* and *The Anti-Christ*, but that you were not that strongly affected; gaining much more inspiration from Tolstoy's *Gospel in Brief*" [see p.36].

Witt: "And then, almost two years after completing the *Tractatus* manuscript, I wrote to a friend, "I have no faith...Let's cut out the transcendental twaddle [or "babble", "idle chatter"] when the whole thing is as plain as a sock on the jaw".

Philo: "Yet after several more years I understand that had all changed".

Witt: And later still, a Methodist minister once asked directly whether I believed in God. I replied: "Yes I do, but the difference between what you believe and what I believe may be infinite".

Also: "Suppose someone said: 'What do you believe, Wittgenstein? Are you a sceptic? Do you know whether you will survive death?' I would really, this is a fact, say 'I can't say. I don't know', because I haven't any clear idea what I'm saying when I'm saying 'I don't cease to exist', etc.". Even in the *Tractatus* I wrote: "God does not reveal himself in the world".

Philo: "One may ask, 'Why the divine hide-and-seek?' God as the Holy Father cannot reveal Himself in the world. – Why not, as omnipotent and miraculous? Jesus as 'Son of man' said: "Render unto Caesar the things that are Caesar's, and unto God the things that are God's" – "and give Me what is mine": thereby affirming complete distinction between One Spirit and worldliness. The world is not to be denied as necessarily limited, only some dynamic world, including individual embodied freewill. We need to respect the relativity of the world, as objective and subjective, and That said to belong to 'Spirit' as personal belief. Even 'Spirit' must relate in at least human conceptual terms – as senseless! None is ever Incomparably Alone. Yet still it may be asked: why is 'Spirit' so lacking in obviousness, allowing so much confusion, doubt and disbelief?"

Nietz: "Life should be ordered on the basis of what is most certain... demonstrable, not as hitherto on that which is most remote, indefinite".

Philo: "– not necessarily all personal life!"

Nietz: "The worst thing is: he ["God"] seems incapable of making himself clearly understood [or "communicating himself clearly"]". That is the fool's and "the divine privilege of being incomprehensible".

I spoke earlier of Epicurus calling the Platonists deceitful Dionysian actors [see p.24], cowardly fleeing from reality into the ideal. And I interpret the religious condition "as hatred of *every* reality, as flight into the 'ungraspable', into the 'inconceivable' (*Unbegreifliche*), as antipathy towards every form, every spatial and temporal concept, towards everything firm, all that is custom...a merely 'inner' world".

Philo: "But it needs to be acknowledged that it is completely wrong, both immoral and mistaken, flight from objective reality to want to see everything only as created from an artistic wilful perspective, as poetic and moral interpretation!"

Witt: "a religious belief could only be...a passionate commitment to a system of reference...It's passionately seizing hold of *this* interpretation".

Philo: "– seizing, moving, reorientating oneself",

Witt: "The problems of life are insoluble on the surface and can only be solved in depth. They are insoluble in surface dimensions".

Philo: "Religious language on the 'surface', as conceptually defined, is essentially senseless, absurd".

Witt: "What gives it ["engulfed" religious thought] depth, however, is its use: the life led by the one who believes it".

Nietz: "The man of faith (*Glaubens*), the 'believer' (*Gläubige*) of every sort is necessarily a dependent man...The believer does not belong to *himself*". "Faith in oneself", on the other hand, admits "one could conceive of such...self-determination, such a freedom of the will that the ["free"] spirit...[is] practised in maintaining himself on insubstantial ropes".

Witt: "An honest (*ehrliche*) religious thinker is like a tightrope walker. He almost looks as though he were walking on nothing but air. His support is the slenderest imaginable. And yet it really is possible to walk on it".

Nonetheless, "skill at playing the game is no longer enough; the question that keeps coming up is...what would be the right game to play?"

Philo: "And there is never any genuine battle for correctness within or between the personal as such. The individual as religious, moral or poetic never knows, never lies and never is correct. For, also to repeat, belief as personal reality relatively completely suspends, puts aside objective reality as knowledge, sense or senselessness. Philosophy of either art, morality or religion describes their concepts as making sense or senseless; whereas knowledge disregards all poetic enchantment, moral sentiment and religious faith. Accordingly, there never is any genuine opposition or conflict between science and religion".

Nietz: I believed: "When one has disclosed [the "passion, error, and self-deception"]...of all existing religions and metaphysical systems, one has refuted them"; and to repeat, "God is thoroughly refuted". However, later I wrote of "*noble* ["victory"]...above...this *underworld* of the ideal ...error...is not refuted – *it freezes*".

Philo: "But one must distinguish metaphysics as essentially mistaken from religion as personal. And only a most hardened heart would try to rule out, fails to admit, others having their personal beliefs.

"Interpretation never recognizes or creates any objective correctness or error. If all were interpretation, how could it be legitimate to say, as you did, 'It is not true, as prejudice would have it, that...'. How could one be critical, even decisive, about anything? Indeed, how could a 'critique of moral values', or evaluation between different moralities, be possible?"

Nietz: "'higher' and 'lower' in morality is not to be measured by a [One] moral yardstick: for there is no absolute Morality (*Moral*)".

Philo "If moral judgment were universally fundamental, conditioned everything, then that would have to mean not to be measured at all!"

Nietz: "we cannot reject the possibility that it ["human intellect"] may include infinite interpretations...but who would feel inclined...to worship...'the Unknown One'? Alas...[there is] too much...foolishness of interpretation...human, all too human folly".

Witt: Again: "Interpretations by themselves do not determine meaning".

Philo (facing Nietzsche): "– including foolishness or wisdom. How can one so hard-heartedly, irresponsibly, immorally and invalidly condemn and limit the essentially unknowing personal inclinations, thoughts and feelings of another, even all others? Moreover, if only interpretation then would not the favouring of instinct for becoming, looking to the future, be yet another tyrannical unhealthy prejudice? You have held that 'to be a lawgiver is a tyranny'; but would that not mean every person as rational must be more or less oppressively harmful to one and all?

"Your view of having to allow infinite realizable perspectives, or interpretations, must allow its criticism in the words you wrote against universal science, and so all knowledge: such so-called 'interpretation... assuming that it is not a mental illness, an idiocy...might therefore still be ...one of the poorest in meaning', and even 'perhaps a pathological state'".

Nietz: "an essentially mechanistic world would be an essentially meaningless world...how absurd would such a 'scientific' estimation [earlier: "interpretation"] of music be!...grasp[ing]...really nothing of what is 'music' in it!"

Philo: "And the same absurdity of excessive science applies to not only art but also religion and morality".

Witt: Yet further, how "to follow a musical phrase with understanding, or to play it with understanding? Don't look inside yourself. Consider rather what makes you say of someone else that this is what he is doing". "This is where religion and art part company".

Philo: "– listening to a composition as created by another person".

Nietz: "at the basis of every religion and morality is ["this imperative"]: 'Do this and this, refrain from this and this – and you will be happy! Otherwise...'".

Witt: "Rules of life...can only serve to describe what we are to do [imperatively], not justify it...Religion says: Do this! – Think like that! – but it cannot justify this...because for every reason it offers there is a valid [or "cogent", *stichhaltigen*] counter-reason".

A religious, aesthetic, or "an ethical proposition is a personal act. Not a statement of fact...the [so-called] justification of an 'ethical proposition' merely attempts to refer the proposition back to others that [are intended to] make an impression on you".

Philo: "Personal persuasion. Subjective experience or perception is always affirmation, believed to be real or true – or falsity – as personal".

Nietz: "knowledge would be in a bad way if it were apportioned to every thinker only as it happened to fit his person!"

Witt: "subjective...[and] objective...betoken a difference between language-games". "Look on the language-game as the *primary* thing. And look on the feelings, etc., as you look on a way of regarding the language-game, as interpretation".

Eternal Recurrence

Nietz: In poetic *"inspiration*...a thought flashes up like lightening, with necessity...I never had any choice. An ecstasy...of freedom". Yet I have also expressed "great admiration for [the ability]...to say something... plainly...clearly, with the reposefulness of the sunlight, not the snatching at effects of a flash of lightning". I even once wrote, a decade later, that: "no trace of *struggle* can be discovered in my life, I am the opposite of an heroic nature...to 'strive' after something, to have a 'goal'...I know none of this from experience...I do not want in the slightest that anything should become other than it is; I do not want myself to become other than I am...But that is how I have always lived. I have harboured no desire".

Philo: "Such untragic will-less quietude, purposeless calm, goes totally against everything you have fervently affirmed about spiritual freedom, the vital need for morality as will to power of ongoing self-overcoming! And that actually means not surrendering to Nature relatively in itself as completely aimless, amoral, indifferent, impersonal objectivity".

Witt: Once more, "is it possible for one so to live that life stops being problematic?"

Nietz: "The great confusion...of psychologists [and I too on this latter occasion] consisted in not distinguishing...two kinds of pleasure – that of falling asleep and that of victory. The exhausted want rest, relaxation, peace, calm...the rich and living want victory". Certainly, "I do not exhort you to peace, but to victory" – "a victory – an overcoming of *oneself*".

Philo: "Accordingly, there is potentially a great ambiguity in a person expressing not wanting anything to be other than it is".

Nietz: Artists know that not every necessity is "painful compelled conformity and constraint...Artists...know...when they cease to act 'voluntarily'...that necessity and 'freedom of will' are then one in them" – "to see as beautiful what is necessary [is]...*Amor fati*".

Philo: "I understand you affirm that artists best 'know' *amor fati*, 'love of fate', or in other words, freewill of necessity".

Nietx: To repeat: "To remain objective...in carrying through an idea – artists succeed best" – "greatness in a human being is *amor fati*: that one wants nothing to be other than it is, not in the future, not in the past, not in all eternity".

Philo (facing Nietzsche): "Thus at last we come to what you call the most uplifting affirmation of all: 'eternal recurrence'. And you related that this idea first came to you amidst the Swiss alpine region in August 1881, when you also mentioned your ecstatic new vision of Zarathustra and 'beyond good and evil' in your poem 'Sils-Maria' [see p.36]".

Nietz: "the idea of eternal recurrence [is] the highest...affirmation that can possibly be attained": "What, if...'This life...you will have to live... innumerable times more; and there will be nothing new in it, but every pain and every joy and every thought and sigh and everything unutterably small or great in your life will have to return to you, all in the same succession' [would this be a "god" or a "demon" speaking?]...The question in each and every thing, 'Do you desire this once more and innumerable times more?'...this ultimate eternal confirmation".

"I, the teacher of the eternal recurrence", introduced this ideal as the hopeful "wish" of the future higher person: "you resist any ultimate peace; you will the eternal recurrence of war and peace...Nobody yet has had this strength!" – "beyond good and evil, and no longer...under the dominion and delusion of [traditional] morality...behold...the ideal of the most world-approving, exuberant, and vivacious man, who...wishes to have it again as it was and is, for all eternity".

"The doctrine of 'eternal recurrence', that is to say of the unconditional and endlessly repeated circular course of all things – this doctrine of [my] Zarathustra *could* possibly already have been taught by Heraclitus".

Philo: "Eternal recurrence as the ultimate hidden harmony was to some extent taught by Pythagoras, but not really by Heraclitus".

Nietz: You refer to "the Pythagoreans...believing that when the constellation of the heavenly bodies is repeated the same things, down to the smallest event, must also be repeated on earth...whenever the stars stand in a certain relation to one another".

Philo: "Yes. Heraclitus to only some extent followed the Pythagoreans in affirming the cosmos of circular becoming as a finite whole eternally revolving. But he maintained eternally destined merely apparent 'just' war of Fiery Becoming. It is Zeus' 'thunderbolt' that 'steers all'; 'conflict [or 'strife', *eris*] is justice' by which inescapable necessity 'all things come to pass', administered by the Furies. The divine Fiery One, Zeus, essentially is prior to, underlies and directs the watery flux of apparent beings, ever-changing self-oppositions. Identity, accordingly, does not completely and really reduce to cyclical opposition: the hidden Fiery Essence perpetually moves all mere appearances. Heraclitus affirms the universe ceaselessly divided against itself, as beginningless and endless 'turnings of fire'; that is, against any eternal returning, the flowing river of Becoming in which nothing ever is the same discrete entity. Heraclitus denies all being as such: that means there never really is anyone who can step into the same non-existent river once, twice or repeatedly as destined ad infinitum!"

Nietz: "Heraclitus will always be right in this, that being is an empty fiction". "Heraclitus [said]: we cannot step into the same river twice. – This is...as true and valid as it ever was".

Philo: "– that most darkly claims, self-defeatingly, to be the ever-fixed, objectively certain single truth that life is only empty fiction!"

Witt: "The man who said that one cannot step into the same river twice said something wrong; one can step into the same river twice". "The truly apocalyptic view of the world is that things do not repeat themselves". Once more: "In order to describe the phenomenon of language, one must describe a practice, not something that happens once".

Philo: "Can one cross the same river twice? The correct answer is "yes and no". Actual meaning needs repeatable public definition; changeable knowledge must have repeatable sense. Repetition without some kind of particular identity – defined sameness – is too general empty abstraction. Each actual individual develops with some ongoing essential identity".

Nietz: "He who has attained to only some degree of freedom of mind cannot feel other than a wanderer on the earth...[as] a final destination... does not exist...[instead taking] pleasure in change" – "we...instinctively attribute a deeper [or "profounder"] meaning and a greater value to becoming and development than we do to what 'is'".

Philo: "That claimed interpretation however, it has to be said, expresses wilful invented prejudice of becoming over being; which means dynamic transient relations privileged over all relatively static structures, identities. Pure relation, without or prior to something that relates to something else, must conceptually actually be empty abstraction".

Nietz: "Becoming as invention...[means] no subject but an action, a positing, creative, no 'causes and effects'"; and again, I have maintained that "all actions are essentially unknown".

Philo: "But actions really determine every meaning in practice!"

Nietz: "must we not all have been here before...and...return eternally?" – "causes of the eternal recurrence...return [all]...to this identical and self-same life...Everything goes, everything returns; the wheel of existence rolls for ever". That is "the Ring of Recurrence".

"That everything recurs [eternally] is the closest approximation of a world of becoming to a world of being". "This world...[is] a sea of forces flowing and rushing together...with an ebb and a flood of its forms... which must return eternally...a becoming...my *Dionysian* world...'beyond good and evil'...*This world is the will to power – and nothing besides!* And you yourselves are also this will to power – and nothing besides!"

Philo (facing Nietzsche): "Your view, even though completely against the religious or metaphysical ideal of timeless Absolute Presence, affirms as the everlasting value, ultimate ideal, the eternal as beginningless and endless circle of time: sameness recurring by universal necessity of causal Fate – inevitably stepping into the same river repeatedly for all time! But causality is no necessity, and a free wilful spirit is 'able *to be different'*".

Nietz: Also as said before, "to interpret and inflate individual personal experiences into universal judgments", that is, "to experience one's own judgment as a universal law...betrays" being part of "inflated, oppressive art that deprives the spirit of its very severity and cheerfulness".

Philo: "Causal connection itself is really always contingent probability, never necessity. To claim universal necessity of actual Fate as causality, or as with the a priori in principle, is nothing but pure abstraction".

Witt: To repeat, "all facts are contingent...of experience...No fact can be necessary, for...negation of [such] a proposition must have sense".

Philo: "Particular experience never yields objective necessity. Again, any such statement of fact must be able to be doubted, denied, conceived as false. And concepts as relatively essential are never contingent facts.

"Each person rational enough for morality must accept responsibility of original willpower for their chosen deeds; and so respect each other's right to enjoy only some freedom of action – which is no Absolute Law. Some freedom must be denied. Anyone's freewill always is limited, as publicly defined in actions: to claim complete universal Freedom, or Fate, is only a false Ideal, a false Idol. Individual freedom from illusory Fate means we all have some real freedom of necessity, to choose and wilfully act, to that extent each creating our own destiny. Freedom is only relative, through making use of some more or less practical fixed structure or rule.

"Once more, necessity as imperative rule-following in actual practice distinguishes senses of being judged as objective conceptual description or personal moral interpretation. Each person lives as an artist expressing some freedom of necessity, rationally recognized in practice, in these two main inter-related ways. The world is essentially our relative world of art and artists – who are creative both subjectively and objectively. Living must mean some ongoing willing, desiring and choosing of subjective as well as objective phenomena creatively, in order to become, to develop".

Witt: "The freedom of the will consists in the fact that future actions cannot be known now".

Philo: "The least, still sure, act of freewill makes the future neither totally uncertain nor totally certain – that makes Fate or omniscience impossible. For what must be chosen, as preordained, would not be a choice; how could even a deity know already what anyone will choose?"

Nietz: Nevertheless: "Joy...wants eternity, wants recurrence, wants everything eternally the same".

Philo (facing Nietzsche): "Each relatively free spirit must be able to choose – able to choose to act – differently. Strong wilful independence is only ever to some extent alone, self-reliant, self-rule. A strong person commands their goal-directed will through life as quite secure in some self-independence, not just following in the wake of another or current of tradition. We all do things more or less freely with some public certainty.

"Different people may consider the idea of eternal recurrence as divine or demonic. You asked for one's 'ultimate eternal confirmation', of this 'most world-approving' ideal, with the opening words 'What, if...' [p.86]. And a free spirit can certainly use the idea of eternal recurrence as if real, to inspire genuine wilful actions as if every action will return eternally".

Epilogue

Philo (facing Nietzsche): "Is it fair to say that you are more of a moral poet than a philosopher?"

Nietz: "With *Ecce Homo* [my distinctive autobiography, at last]...I've settled the question of who I am once and for all. Henceforth no one should be concerned with me, but only with the reasons why I am here".

Witt: And again, any philosophical reasons are "further descriptions".

Nietz: "Am I a philosopher? Who cares?" – yet still to reiterate further: "I...understand myself as the first *tragic philosopher*", relating "my new philosophy". "One seeks [to create] a...philosophy" for "real [or "proper", *eigentlicher*] *power* of spirituality, real *depth* of spiritual insight, in short [means] philosophy" – "philosophers...traverse the whole range of human values...and make it clear". Such "a philosophy...has thereby alone placed itself beyond good and evil". Thus, for example, my book *Twilight of the Idols, or: How to Philosophize with a Hammer* means "*new philosophers* ...[need to] teach...a revaluation of values" – that is "the future task of the philosopher".

Philo: "You interpret yourself as a new moral and poetic 'philosopher' and speak of your 'philosophy', all the while emphasizing the philosopher as person. Yet, strictly, only statements are true or false. Truth and falsity directly belong to no person as such but to language, expressing shareable personal or public kinds of reality or unreality – essentially recognized as such by people, who are each responsible for their statements made".

Witt: Also once more: "Practice gives the words their sense" – "it is the particular use of a word only which gives the word its meaning...The use of the word *in practice* is its meaning".

Nietz: "being fair...demands much practice and good will, and very much very good sense" – "the only possible right way: through practice".

Philo: "An insisted conviction about objectivity never guarantees not being wholly misguided. Not always doing what's right, great individuals express great mistakes. There is no greater teacher than mistake!

(facing Nietzsche) "Practice as itself objective is never interpretation. You have spoken of 'objectivity', 'knowledge' and 'conceptual sense' in 'practice', but with a total absence of admitting any genuine objectivity! Accordingly, it has to be honestly recognized that you have blundered in everything objective – muddling, indeed denying, everything really objective – in addition expressing vain, contemptuous, slanderous, dark, immoral wilful misjudgment of objectivity relatively entirely in itself!

"A complete distinction needs to be admitted between facts, or rational necessities, objectively given and personal perspectives or interpretations.

Morality as such must be subjective evaluation not objective. Even so, any realizable meaning, whether objective or subjective, is essentially conceptually so called, as certainly objectively defined".

Witt: That again is "a consensus of action...not...opinion".

Philo "And rational recognition of any statement as such essentially accepts, even though objectively unjustifiably, participation in that rule-governed language, at least relative to everyday public practice. Every statement is actually recognized by someone, more or less consciously, as defined. Each participant in rational language needs to obey its certain rules of meaning, thereby avoiding being disrespectful to every follower and to those conceptual kinds of rules.

(facing Nietzsche:) "Despite your claims to the contrary – indeed they actually show – you have not entirely given up the genuinely objective outlook. Your every statement, including of 'tragic wisdom', is conveyed using rational language. But as an ascetic kind of idealist in relation to objectivity – that is, held fast in your own wilful apparent universal self-captivating net of perspectival interpretative convictions – you have failed to acknowledge explicitly any objectivity relatively in itself as genuine, so also any essential distinction between the objectively creative rule-giver and the subjectively creative artist. To claim to see through, or abolish, all genuine objective reality must be self-deceiving objective mistake; even to deny rational practice depends on accepting it. To condemn everything as mere appearance is not only false statement but also harmful. To call all the world a poem or moral is really a 'beautiful or noble blunder', that is, both immoral prejudicial desire and senseless mistake. Your claims to 'only interpretation' only genuinely apply to subjective expressions, as always objectively defined. Nothing objective, correct or mistaken is ever interpretation, morality or poetry as such".

Witt: "Nothing is more important for teaching us to understand the concepts we have than constructing fictitious ones". Once more, "to remove some trouble caused in someone's mind...our method is not merely to enumerate actual usages of words, but rather deliberately to invent new ones, some of them because of their absurd appearance".

Philo (again facing Nietzsche): "I remarked earlier that what you say of 'the philosopher' needs to be taken to mean only 'the philosopher as moral' [see p.62], conveying defined moral values – yet emphasized with philosophy and science, all objectivity, as such relatively aside. For your statements made about poetic morality really are tragic, uplifting but also disastrous. You consider yourself a moral poet-philosopher, yet you are rightly much more of a moral poet than a philosopher. You claim that all philosophy is fundamentally moral 'personality' [see p.61], with all the traditional philosophers seduced by Circe; but none has been beguiled by the need – and ambiguity – of moral rules to greater excess than you! For morality as always personal evaluation never defines any rule in practice.

"It has to be honestly said, Nietzsche, all your claims to philosophical, conceptual, truth are objectively mistaken! For philosophy as correct, or mistaken, is never interpretation. Revaluation of only moral interpretation really means such subjectivity defined by concepts as known by example. Despite your actual behaviour, you failed utterly, in any explicit way, to admit overcoming yourself as claimed only interpreter, that is, to admit overcoming your will to only moral poetic power! The great and right value of your teaching as philosopher of morality is nothing you claim to interpret as 'objective' – but remains your expressing morality as personal, proclaiming the need for noble ongoing self-overcoming, especially free from ascetic ideals turned against life. For extreme ascetics, in so-called 'selfless' but really self-captivating subjective conviction, curse this life by wilfully holding on to an imagined unrealizable Ideal, never able to be approached by wilful action. Thoughts are only dreams until acted out; every genuine ideal is realizable, attainable through some real actions".

Nietzsche silently smiled.

Witt: "I realized...The best that I could write would never be more than philosophical remarks". "It is difficult to paint an adequate picture of... [grammatical] description...And after all a painter is basically what I am".

Philo: "– and not so much a poet as an artist describing objective use of concepts, various kinds of sense or senselessness in practice, which as emphasizing objectivity is the skilful unpoetic art of philosophy".

Witt: "My main movement of thought is a completely different one today from...years ago. And this is similar to when a painter makes a transition from one school to another". "It suddenly seemed to me that I should publish those old thoughts [of the *Tractatus*] and the new ones together: that the latter could be seen in the right light only by contrast with and against the background of my old way of thinking". Also: "I should not like my writing to spare other people the trouble of thinking. But, if possible, to stimulate someone to thoughts of his own".

Philo: "Thought can compare different kinds of meanings, nonetheless in correct philosophy, conceptual descriptions, there is nothing to think!"

Witt: Certainly, to repeat, "'obeying a rule' is a practice. And to *think* one is obeying a rule is not to obey a rule".

Philo: "A further key distinction needing to be recognized is between subjective and objective senses of creativity. Relative freedom to will any meaning so called must involve some objective concept creation.

(facing Wittgenstein) "You eventually, showing great integrity, came to recognize the representational logically atomic system of the *Tractatus* as conceptually mistaken. After that metaphysical invention of unrealizable idealistic imagination, however, you kept stressing the need for clarifying philosophy to destroy, over its dynamically articulating sense in practice. It has to be said, Wittgenstein, you strictly neglected to make explicit the furthering of objective understanding by the creation of concepts as such.

91

The whole system of the *Tractatus* retracted, your later philosophical statements lack sufficient recognition of the philosopher's essential role in describing relatively new linguistic practices, or 'language-games': including objectively creating, improving everyday sense – not merely given, nor emphasized as simplified, absurdity or senseless ideal".

Wittgenstein silently smiled.

Philo: "Philosophy only describes statements determined by relative definitions, emphasized as consisting of conceptual kinds of necessity – also essentially illustrated by known factual reference – in objectively certain practice. The philosopher's descriptions communicated either create confusion, or clarify given concepts, or create new concepts.

"Talking with the two of you makes it clear that philosophy is correctly neither creating concepts of a discredited, in a sense sceptical, objectivity of claimed perspectival interpretation, nor only clarifying already given concepts. The philosopher's rational right task is essentially twofold: to articulate some objective sense or senselessness of objective and moral imperatives; that is, to describe some conceptual necessities clarifying statements made, as well as to create concepts, which must include wilful evaluations of personal moral necessity as conceptually defined.

"Relative linguistic freedom to will meaning needs to involve creating genuinely objectively, that is, making some new conceptual connections to define new meanings, to develop and improve recognition of rational practices. And anyone sufficiently rational must combine conceptual rules with responsibility for their choices made, as guided by defined personal moral rules – not least some essential concepts of individual higher self.

"The vital purpose of every individual embodied life is to live creating purpose. Each human being essentially acts as willing artist and evaluator – a creator, preserver and destroyer – of subjective and objective values. Moral life is created by rational individuals as necessity: to live one must consciously, boldly, even gratefully, continue – by means of conceptual and moral certainties in practice – to will to choose something life-giving, strengthening, inspiring, elevating, for which it is worthwhile to live.

"The moral poet and the philosopher can never contradict each other. There is no genuine conflict, or dispute, between them – unless the poet and the philosopher went to cuffs in the question! – for any so-called fight between the two would be completely confused opposition: nothing really certainly recognized as personal or impersonal. Never genuine opponents, the two accompany one another hand in hand.

"Distinguished gentlemen, through your works of such very different emphasis, Friedrich Nietzsche as poetic and morally re-evaluating and the later Ludwig Wittgenstein as philosophically objective, I must say you complement one another wonderfully! Each in your kind and wise way, I thank you, wholeheartedly, for conveying so much highly inspirational twofold clear certainty of moral and conceptual insights".

Main Bibliography
and Abbreviations

Nietzsche

BT   *The Birth of Tragedy out of the Spirit of Music*, written between summer 1870 and winter 1871, published January 1872, translated by Whiteside, 1993, Penguin; including also the 1886 Preface 'Attempt at a Self-Criticism'. Translation of *Dionysische* as 'Dionysiac' is replaced here by 'Dionysian'.

UM   *Untimely Meditations*, written from 1872 to summer 1875: I 'David Strauss' (1873), II On History (1874), III 'Schopenhauer as educator' (1874), IV 'Richard Wagner in Bayreuth' (1876) - translated by Hollingdale 1983, Cambridge University Press.

PTAG   'Philosophy during the Tragic Age of the Greeks', 1873 unfinished, translated by Mügge 1911, in *Early Greek Philosophy & Other Essays* (New York 1964) - also

TFUS   including 'On Truth and Falsity [or 'Lies'; *Lüge*] in their ultramoral [*aussermoralischen*] Sense', 1873-74 essay posthumously published, translated by Mügge.

HH   *Human, All Too Human*, started in summer 1876, published May 1878, translated by Faber and Lehmann 1984, Penguin 1994; or where indicated translated by Hollingdale, 1986,

AOM   Cambridge UP - 'with two supplements': *Assorted Opinions and Maxims*, written in 1878, published 1879 and *The*

WS   *Wanderer and His Shadow*, written in 1879, published 1880 - both translated by Hollingdale 1986, Cambridge UP.

D   *Daybreak* (*Morgenröte*), written in 1880-81, published 1881, translated by Hollingdale, 1997, Cambridge UP.

GS   *The Gay Science*, first edition written from 1881 to 1st July 1882, published autumn 1882, enlarged 1887 (Book 5, §343-§383, written in late 1886 after BGE), translated by Kaufmann 1974, Vintage Books edition, Random House.

TSZ   *Thus Spoke Zarathustra*, 1883-85 (Part IV finished by early February 1885; second printing in 1892 was its first publicly) translated by Hollingdale 1961, reprinted 1971, Penguin.

WTP   *The Will to Power*, a compilation from notebooks 1883-88, posthumously published in 1901 and expanded several times, first (by some 200 pages) in 1904, and also in the 1911 edition; edited by Kaufmann, translated by Kaufmann and Hollingdale 1968, Vintage Books edition, Random House.

BGE	*Beyond Good and Evil*, written from summer 1885 to winter 1885-86, published 1886, translated by Hollingdale 1973, 1990 Penguin; or where indicated translated by Zimmern, 1906, then in Nietzsche's Complete Works edition from 1909.
GM	*On the Genealogy of Morals*, written in July 1887, published that year, translated by D. Smith, 1996, Oxford UP.
TI	*Twilight of the Idols*, written from June to September 1888, published late January 1889 - in the edition used bound with -
AC	*The Anti-Christ*, written in September 1888, published 1895; both translated by Hollingdale, 1968, Penguin.
EH	*Ecce Homo*, written in October 1888, published 1908, translated by Hollingdale, 1979, Penguin.
SPL	*Nietzsche: A Self-Portrait from His Letters*, translated by Fuss and Shapiro 1971, Harvard University Press.

Wittgenstein

'Notes on Logic, [October] 1913' (given as Appendix I in *Wittgenstein's 'Notebooks 1914-1916'*).
'Notes Dictated to G. E. Moore in Norway, April 1914' (Appendix II in *Wittgenstein's 'Notebooks 1914-1916'*).
Wittgenstein's 'Notebooks 1914-1916' edited by von Wright and Anscombe, 1961, second edition 1979, Blackwell.

| T | *Tractatus Logico-Philosophicus*, written during 1913-18, published in German 1921, translated by Ogden and Ramsey, 1922, Routledge; or where indicated translated by Pears and McGuinness, 1961. |

'Some Remarks on Logical Form', article in *Proceedings of the Aristotelian Society, Supplementary* volume IX, 1929.
'A Lecture on Ethics', delivered to the Heretics Society in Cambridge on 17.11.1929, published in *Philosophical Review*, volume 74, 1965, pp.3-12.
Philosophical Remarks, composed during 1929-32, German edition 1965; translated by Hargreaves, 1975, Blackwell.

| LWVC | *Ludwig Wittgenstein and the Vienna Circle*, 1929-1932, conversations recorded (in shorthand notebooks) by Waismann, edited by McGuinness, translated by Schulte and McGuinness 1979, Blackwell. |
| PG | *Philosophical Grammar* (part of "The Big Typescript", written from 1930 until mainly 1934), published in German 1969; edited by Rhees, translated by Kenny, 1974, Blackwell. |

TBT	'Philosophy', a prospective chapter, pp.406-435, of "The Big Typescript", written from 1930 until mainly 1934, translated by Kenny, also given in *The Wittgenstein Reader*, Blackwell, 1994, pp.263-79; otherwise quoted as indicated from the translation given with the German text in *Philosophical Occasions*, edited by Klagge and Nordmann, 1993, Hackett, pp.160-199.
	Ludwig Wittgenstein: Public and Private Occasions, edited by Klagge and Nordmann, 2003, Rowman & Littlefield: consisting of *Diaries* 1930-32, 1936-37, correspondence with Hänsel, and various reports of lectures and discussions.
Lectures 1930-32	*Wittgenstein's Lectures, Cambridge 1930-1932*: from the notes of J. King and D. Lee, edited by Lee, 1980, Blackwell.
Lectures 1930-33	'Wittgenstein's Lectures in 1930-33' notes by G. E. Moore, in *Mind* January 1954 (volume LXIII, pp.1-15; on lectures 1930), July 1954 (volume LXIII, pp.289-316; on lectures 1930-31) and January 1955 (volume LXIV, pp.1-27; on lectures 1932-33).
Lectures 1932-35 YB	*Wittgenstein's Lectures, Cambridge 1932-1935*: from the notes of A. Ambrose and M. Macdonald, edited by Ambrose, 1979, Blackwell: including 'The Yellow Book' lectures (from the notes of Ambrose) Part I, pp.43-55, 1933 (preceding BlB) and Part II, pp.56-73, 1933-34 (contemporary with BlB).
BlB, BrB	*The Blue and Brown Books*, 1958, Blackwell: consisting of notes made from Wittgenstein's dictation in English to close friends and pupils during 1934-35 (*Blue* pp.1-74, 1933-34, *Brown* pp.77-185, 1934-35).
PESD	'Notes for Lectures on "Private Experience" and "Sense Data", c.1935, *Philosophical Review*, 77, 1968, pp.271-320. Notes for 'Philosophy Lecture' possibly originally 1935-36 then revised for - but in the end withdrawn as - the British Academy lecture of 1942; published in *Philosophical Occasions*, edited by Klagge and Nordmann, 1993, Hackett.
PI	*Philosophical Investigations*, from the period 1929-50, written mainly during 1933-46, published 1953, translated by Anscombe, 1968, Blackwell.
RFM	*Remarks on the Foundations of Mathematics*, written mainly during 1937-44, edited by von Wright, Rhees and Anscombe, translated by Anscombe, 1956, Blackwell.
LRB	*Lectures on Religious Belief*, c.1938, in *Lectures and Conversations on Aesthetics, Psychology and Religious Belief*, consisting of notes made by Wittgenstein's hearers, edited by Barrett, 1966, Blackwell.

LFM	*Wittgenstein's Lectures on the Foundations of Mathematics, Cambridge 1939*, edited by Diamond, 1976, Harvester (quotations given are of notes made by his hearers).
	Zettel, fragments from 1929 but mainly 1945-48, edited by Anscombe and von Wright, translated by Anscombe, 1967, second edition 1981, Blackwell.
	Remarks on the Philosophy of Psychology, written during 1946-49, volume I edited by Anscombe and von Wright, translated by Anscombe, 1980, Blackwell; volume II edited by von Wright and Nymann, translated by Luckhardt and Aue, 1980, Blackwell.
OC	*On Certainty*, written during 1949-51, published 1969, edited by Anscombe and von Wright, translated by Paul and Anscombe, 1975, Blackwell.
CV	*Culture and Value*, a selection from Wittgenstein's notebooks of 1929-51 (and one note from 1914), edited by von Wright, first published as *Vermischte Bemerkungen* ('Miscellaneous Remarks') in 1977; revised second edition translated by Winch 1980, amended 1998, Blackwell.

References

Prologue

p.1   N: 'To stay cheerful', TI Foreword, 1888.
      W: 'The highest...that I am prepared', *Diaries* 13.2.1937.
      N: 'The questions as to the beginning', PTAG §1.
      W: 'Language contains the same traps', CV 1931, so too TBT §90.
      'As little philosophy as I have read', manuscript 135, 27.7.1947.
      'Reading numbs my soul', *Diaries* 13.2.1931. 'I believe it might
      interest a philosopher', OC §387.
      N: 'I know my fate', EH, 'Why I am a Destiny' §1. *'Beyond Good
      and Evil*...People will *dare* read it', letter to von Meysenbug,
      24.9.1886, in SPL.

The Birth of Tragedy out of the Spirit of Music

p.2   N: 'I shall fix my gaze', BT §16 – 'the two gods of art', BT §1.
      'what an *impossible* book', BT 1886 Preface §2 – 'with this
      questionable book...I called it the *Dionysian*', BT 1886 Preface
      §5. Note that the translation of *Dionysische* as 'Dionysiac' is
      replaced throughout the text here by 'Dionysian'.
      'I was concerned with nothing except', WTP §1050, 1888 –
      'Dionysian art of music', BT §1 – *'tragedy arose from the tragic
      chorus*', BT §7. 'Later, the attempt is made', BT §8.
      'The satyr...this man of the woods', BT §8 condensed text.
      'Singing and dancing', BT §1 – 'the Dionysian...mystical
      sense', BT§2, capital letter added for 'Unity', *Einheit*.
      'I should believe only', TSZ I 'Of Reading and Writing'.
      'phenomena we are...[is] an illusion', BT §4 – 'Apollo, the
      interpreter of dreams', BT §4.
p.3   'Only as an aesthetic phenomenon', BT §5 and §24 – 'beauty
      triumphs', BT §16.
      'art – and *not* morality', BT 1886 Preface §5. In 'longing for
      the primal', BT §8 – 'longing for...redemption...['entirely
      thoughtless', BT 1886 Preface §5] and contradictory', BT §4,
      capital letters added for 'Truly' and 'Existent' – 'floating in the
      purest bliss', BT §4 – 'in...the aesthetic, purely contemplative',
      BT §6 – 'and we might even describe Apollo', BT §1.
      'Dionysian...will...[means] the eternal life', BT §16 – 'join the
      Dionysian procession', BT §20. 'Here, in the highest artistic
      symbolism', BT §4: 'The best of all things', BT §3; this

quotation given by Nietzsche follows Theognis 'Elegies' line 425, and Sophocles *Oedipus at Colonus* line 1225.

W: 'In art it is hard', CV c.1932-34.
'And the beautiful is', *Notebooks*, 21.10.1916.
'When we have no criterion of correctness', PI §258.

N: 'But all life is dispute', TSZ II 'Of the Sublime Men'.
'Because...most of us are bad poets', BT §8.

P: 'such stuff as dreams are made', quoting Shakespeare, *The Tempest*, 4.1, Prospero.

p.4 W: 'I cannot seriously', OC §676 – 'if I am dreaming', OC §383.

P: 'It is a dream! I want to dream on!', BT §1.

N: 'the Greeks, who revealed the profound mysteries', BT §1.

W: 'There is, indeed, the inexpressible', T 6.522.

N: 'the *mystery doctrine*', BT §10, capital letters added for 'Unity' and 'Oneness', both *Einheit* – 'in tragedy...Dionysus speaks', BT §21.
'How I now regret', BT 1886 Preface §6 – 'beneath the heaviness', BT 1886 Preface §3. '*The Birth of Tragedy*...smells offensively Hegelian', EC on BT §1.
'sit peacefully', BT §4.

p.5 'veil of Maya. Just as the boatman sits in his small boat, trusting his frail craft in a stormy sea...rising and falling with the howling, mountainous waves, so in the midst of a world full of suffering and misery the individual man calmly sits, supported by and trusting the *principium individuationis*', BT§1, quoting Schopenhauer, *The World as Will and Representation*, volume I, §63, pp.352-53.
'Dionysian...will...[means] the eternal', BT §16; quoted on p.3.

W: 'I cannot bend the happenings', *Notebooks*, 11.6.1916. 'The world is independent of my will', ibid, 5.7.1916; also T 6.373. 'There is really only one world soul', ibid, 23.5.1915. 'And in this sense', ibid, 17.10.1916.
'Aesthetically, the miracle is', ibid, 20.10.1916. 'Not how the world is', T 6.44-45.

N: 'Apollo I [did] see', BT §16, capital added for 'Redemption', *Erlösung*.
'the highest artistic symbolism', BT §4.

p.6 '*Apollinian – Dionysian*...antithesis', WTP §798, 1888.
'timidly...[like] a dainty', BT §8.
'life is at bottom indestructibly powerful', BT §7. '*Dionysus* of the Greeks', WTP 1052, 1888 – 'in...eternity...in Dionysian ecstasy', BT §17, capital added for 'Living thing', *Lebendige*.
'The individual must be consecrated', UM IV §4 – 'sacrifice with me in the temple of both deities!', BT §25.

'beyond the phenomenal world', BT §16, capital letters added for 'Life of the Will', *Leben des Willens*.
'Dionysus cut to pieces', WTP §1052, 1888.

W: 'The temporal immortality', T 6.4312.

p.7 N: 'the illusion of illusion', BT §4.
'The misunderstanding of passion', WTP §387, 1888 – 'vision of the most afflicted ['suffering']...only in (*nur im*) *illusion*', BT 1886 Preface §5 – 'life is something essentially amoral', ibid, §5 – 'nature's cruelty', BT §7, so too 'natural cruelty' §18.
'in the highest artistic symbolism', BT §4.

p.8 'poetry...wishes to be...and the lie [or 'falsity'] of culture (*Culturlüge*)', BT §8.

W: 'Wishing is not acting', *Notebooks*, 4.11.1916. 'The will seems always to have', ibid, 4.11.1916.

N: 'the entire [first] book', BT, 1886 Preface §5 – 'a cruel, savage daemon', BT 9.
'Dionysian release', BT §21 – 'a mystical sense of Unity', BT §2, capital letter added for 'Unity', *Einheit* – 'mystical...Being', BT §16. 'The word '*Dionysian*' means', WTP §1050, 1888.

W: 'No sign leads us beyond itself', PG §71.

N: 'symbolism of music', BT §6.

p.9 ''illusion' here is the reflection', BT §4.
'illusion...as a continuous becoming in time', BT §4. 'Dionysian Reality', BT §7 (capital letter added for 'Reality') of selfless 'Being', BT §16, as 'the Truly Existent, the primal Oneness', BT §4 (capital letters added for 'Truly' and 'Existent'), 'the One Real (*der eine wharhaft reale*) Dionysus', BT §10 (capital letters added for 'One' and 'Real').
'looking away', BT §4 – 'the highest artistic symbolism', BT §4.
'tragedies have to do with', AOM §23 – '*the tragic*. The Greeks ...misunderstood it', WTP §1029, 1884-86. 'Aristotle's great misunderstanding...that one is "purged"' of 'two *depressive* affects', both WTP §851, 1888.
'precocious', BT 1886 Preface §2.

W: 'I will call 'will' first', *Notebooks*, 21.7.1916. 'What is good and evil', ibid, 5.8.1916. 'Good and evil only enter', ibid, 2.8.1916.

p.10 N: ''*Apollinian*' means: the urge to perfect self-sufficiency', WTP §1050, 1888. 'Alas, my friends', GS §340.
'Dionysus is a philosopher', BGE §295.
'who runs the risk of longing...[and 'yearning for the Void', BT §21, capital letter added for 'Void', *Nichts*]...the terrible truth ['nature's cruelty...the horror and absurdity of existence', BT §7, condensed text; similarly §18], outweighs every motive', BT §7 – 'the aesthetic, purely contemplative will-less state', BT §6.

P: 'In your book...art is not yet emphasized explicitly as error (*Irrthümer*) or lie (*Lüge*) but called illusion (*Schein*) of illusion'.

p.11   N: 'within the context of', BT 1886 Preface §2.
'the task...*to see science*', ibid,§2 – 'the book...[is] presented', ibid, §2. 'Only as an aesthetic', BT §5 and §24; quoted on p.3.

W: 'further descriptions', Lectures 1930-33, reported by Moore, *Mind* volume LXIV, p.19.

N: 'again...I find...[my] book', BT 1886 Preface §3.

W: 'unshakeable belief...will show', LRB, I, p.54.

N: 'the older Hellenic instinct', TI, 'What I Owe to the Ancients', §§4-5 condensed text.

p.12   'morality...[as] a 'will to the denial of life'', BT 1886 Preface §5.
''Eternal bliss': psychological nonsense', WTP §579, 1883-88.
'Truly, nothing could be...absolute Standards', BT 1886 Preface §5, capital letter added for 'Standards', *Maassen*.
'a youthful work...a 'first book'', ibid, §2.

Tractatus Logico-Philosophicus

p.13   N: 'I contend that there has never been', HH §253.

W: 'I don't believe I have ever invented', CV 1931 – although 'in Norway during the year', CV 1931.

N: 'Our usual...observation...imagines', WS §11.

W: 'An entire mythology', TBT §93, translated in *Philosophical Occasions*, p.199. 'People are deeply embedded', TBT §90, translated in *Philosophical Occasions*, p.185 – 'We must plough', TBT §92, translated in *Philosophical Occasions*, p.195.

N: 'As is so often the case', HH §14.

W: 'Our language is constructed', YB §2.
'Don't get involved in partial problems', *Notebooks*, 1.11.1914.
'The great problem', ibid, 1.6.1915.

p.14   'I finished the book', letter to Russell 13.3.1919. 'When I wrote that', discussion 29.7.1941, reported by Thouless, quoted in *Ludwig Wittgenstein: Public and Private Occasions*, p.387.
'The simplest proposition', T 4.21. 'The propositions which represent this ultimate', 'Some Remarks on Logical Form', 1929 article – 'the understanding of general propositions', 'Notes on Logic, 1913', similarly T 4.411.
'none of our experience', *Notebooks*, 12.8.1916, also T 5.634.
'There are no necessary facts', Lectures 1930-32, C XIII, 1931-32, p.93. 'Philosophical problems are not solved', 'Philosophy' lecture §1, 1932 – 'existence and non-existence', *Zettel* §364.
'It is the essence of philosophy', Lectures 1932-35, X, 1934,

p.97. 'The object [or 'aim', *Der Zweck*] of philosophy', T 4.112 – 'as always, the a priori certain proves', T 6.3211. 'Logic must take care of itself', T 5.473. 'Logic is prior to every experience', T 5.552, trans. Pears and McGuinness – 'logic is a priori', T 5.4731. 'Logic is not a theory', T 6.13 – 'the all-embracing world-mirroring logic', *Notebooks*, 24.1.1915, likewise T 5.511. 'A proposition is [only] a description', Lectures 1930-32, B IX, §1, 1931. 'To understand a proposition means to know', T 4.024. 'A proposition...is a picture', T 4.03 – of realizable 'positive... [or] negative fact', T 2.06. 'A picture contains the possibility', T 2.203, trans. Pears and McGuinness. 'A logical picture of facts is a thought', T 3, trans. Pears and McGuinness. 'Propositions... cannot represent what they', T 4.12-4.121 – 'we know a priori', T 6.33. 'A picture can represent every reality', T 2.171-2 – 'A proposition shows its sense', T 4.022.

'My propositions are elucidatory...nonsensical (*unsinnig*) [translated by Ogden inaccurately as 'senseless']', T 6.54.

p.15   'What is essential', Lectures 1930-32, B IV, §4, 1930. 'What can be shown cannot be said', T 4.1212 – 'the inexpressible...shows itself', T 6.522. 'Whereof one cannot speak', T 7.

N: 'For me they were steps', TI, 'Maxims and Arrows', 42 (and Wittgenstein read TI from 1914, see p.36) – 'in certain cases', end of 1886 Preface to HH.

W: 'the point of the book is ethical', unused draft for the *Tractatus* Preface; stated in an undated, almost definitely November 1919, letter to its potential but baffled publisher von Ficker – 'the truth of the thoughts', T Preface. 'On all [philosophical] questions', Lectures 1932-35, X, Michaelmas term 1934, p.97.

'no language is conceivable', *Philosophical Remarks* §47; also TBT §91. 'Grammar is a mirror', Lectures 1930-32, A IV, §3, 1930. 'Grammar is not the expression', ibid, A V, §1, 1930. 'Grammar is a description', ibid, Notes, p.115. 'No description ...can justify', ibid, B VIII, §3, 1931. 'You cannot justify grammar', ibid, B X, §5, 1931.

'Language is connected with reality', ibid, A VII, §1, 1930. 'I have been forced to recognize', PI Preface, 1945.

p.16   "plunge into something terrible" to "put straight", "put correctly", having been "misled" by the expressions "sense" and "nonsense", Lectures 1930-33, said towards the end of the Lent – January to March – term Lectures, 1933; reported by Moore, *Mind* volume LXIII, p,295.

N: 'Nothing is rarer', WTP §445, 1888.

W: 'It is characteristic of obsessions', Lectures 1932-25, X, Michaelmas term 1934, p.99.

N: 'Scientific philosophy', HH §131, 1876-78.

W: 'the pretence is that', CV 1937. 'The philosopher is a man', RFM, IV §53; likewise CV 1944. 'There is not *a* philosophical method', PI §133.

N: 'art...is presented as the properly *metaphysical*', BT 1886 Preface §5; quoted on p.3.

W: 'Philosophers constantly see', BlB, p.18, 1933 – 'our ['philosophical'] considerations', PI §109. 'My fundamental ideas', said to Drury in 1948, *Recollections of Wittgenstein*, ed. Rhees, OUP, 1984, p.158. 'In philosophy there are no deductions', 'Notes on Logic, 1913'.

p.17 'Philosophy is not a theory', T 4.112. 'Grammatical conventions cannot be justified', *Philosophical Remarks* §7.

N: 'That impulse towards', TFUS – 'our intellect is a mirror', D §121 – 'depersonalization...objective man', BGE §207 – 'every great philosophy', UM III §3.
'Science...pounces', PTAG §3.

W: 'For there seemed to pertain', PI §89. That 'can lead us', PI §81. 'Frege and Russell made up', YB §15. 'I myself spoke of', PG Appendix 4B, probably 1936 addition – 'in the calculus I once described', PG, Appendix 4A, 1932. 'At the root of all this', PG Appendix 4B, probably 1936 addition – 'what we call logic', Lectures 1932-35, 'Philosophy' §11, 1932-33.

P: 'A...sign...*expresses* its sense...[and] *designates* its meaning', quoting Frege, 'On Sense and Meaning', in *Collected Papers on Mathematics, Logic and Philosophy*, p.161.

W: 'Frege appealed to', T 6.1271. 'Self-evidence of which Russell', T 5.4731. 'In the course of our conversations', CV 1937.

p.18 N: 'the prototype of *theoretical man*', BT §15.

W: 'A characteristic of [so-called] theorists', *Diaries* 6.5.1931.

N: 'no *a priori* truths', WTP §862, 1884 – such claims 'are not forms of knowledge', WTP §530, 1883-88 – 'the most general, the emptiest concepts', TI, "Reason' in Philosophy' §4.

W: 'What I am opposed to', CV 19.8.1940.

Circe, Socrates and Plato

p.19 W: 'A definition surely serves', PI §258 – 'we take as the criterion', LFM, XIX. 'But...a picture', PG §100; also *Zettel* §236.
'one might explain the word', LFM, XX – 'the way we live', LFM, XXVI.

N: 'guided by Apollo', BT §4. 'But morality...knows', D 1886 Preface §3 – 'faith in morality', ibid, §1.

'a struggle...against the subordination', TI, 'Expeditions of an Untimely Man' §24.

'the Circe of philosophers', WTP §461, 1888 – 'The Circe of mankind', EH, 'Why I Write Such Good Books' §5.

P: 'or some enchanted trifle' (Alonso), 'that will not let you believe things certain' (Prospero); 'I'll drown my book' (Prospero), quoting Shakespeare, *The Tempest*, 5.1.

p.20 W: 'Philosophy is a battle', PI §109.

N: 'We must stride boldly', BT §16.

Tyrants of the spirit, HH §261 – 'the war of the opposites', PTAG §5 – 'such a wonderfully idealised company', PTAG §1. 'the older Greeks felt differently', D §38. 'These philosophers... were tyrants', HH §261.

'I set apart with high reverence', TI, "Reason' in Philosophy', §2 – 'he denied "Being"', PTAG §5. 'Everything...is in a state', PTAG, Notes §7 – 'the play of the great world-child', PTAG §8 – 'the eternally living fire', PTAG §7 – 'all Becoming...the divergence', PTAG §5 – 'desire compels the artist to create', PTAG §7. 'Only as an aesthetic phenomenon', BT §5 and §24.

W: 'The work of art', *Notebooks*, 7.10.1916.

P: It is Zeus' 'thunderbolt' that 'steers all', 'conflict [or 'strife', *eris*] is justice', by which 'all things come to pass', as administered by the Furies (fragments 41, 80, 94) – 'turnings of fire' (fragment 31). Hesiod had distinguished Strife as cruel or healthy competitive striving (*Works and Days* 11-26).

p.21 N 'dived into the cold bath...['as a resting, dead ball', §17]... bloodless as an abstraction', PTAG §10 – 'for Parmenides "Being"', PTAG §12 – 'death-like rest', PTAG §11.

P: 'Alone, unmoving...being [or 'Being', *einai*]' (fragment 53).

W: 'If by eternity is understood', T 6.4311. 'But is it possible for one', *Notebooks*, 6.7.1916.

N: 'The One, [means] flight', PTAG, Notes §8, 'Conclusion'. 'Socrates...and what indeed did he do', BGE §191.

p.22 W: 'Reading the Socratic dialogues', CV 30.7.1931. 'Socrates keeps reducing the sophist', CV 1947. 'A definition surely serves', PI §258. 'I need a criterion of identity', PI §288.

N: 'led by instinctive moral definitions', WTP §407, 1884 – 'no *criterion of truth*', WTP §516, 1887-88.

W: 'I call 'symptom' a phenomenon', BIB, pp.25-28, 1933, condensed text.

"sense" is not "sharply bounded" (said towards the end of the Lent, January to March, term Lectures, 1933), "'sense' is vague", Lectures 1930-33, reported by Moore, *Mind* volume LXIII, p.295. Sense is 'a concept with blurred edges', PI §71.

p.23   'Socrates fails', Lectures 1932-35, X, Michaelmas term 1934, p.96. 'I cannot give a full', CV 1949.

P: Pythagoreans...only symbolically killed the 'traitor' who revealed the 'irrationality' of numbers, by inscribing his name on a tomb (see Iamblichus, *On the Pythagorean Way of Life*, trans. Dillon and Hershbell, 1991, Scholars Press, pp.246-47). So the drowning may express a soul adrift with no standard of measurement (see Pappus, *Commentary on Euclid* 10.1.1, c.AD 300). For some more details on this 'irrational' see the author's *Oneself the Mystic and Philosopher*, pp.129-131.

N: 'those old sages from Thales', PTAG §1 – 'the philosophers are the *décadents*', TI, 'What I Owe to the Ancients' §3 – 'that which brought about', BT 1886 Preface §1.

p.24   'Might the scientific approach', ibid, §1 – 'at the last moment of his life...he said: "O Crito, I owe Asclepius a rooster" [Plato's *Phaedo*, 118]...Socrates *suffered life*!', GS §340.

'Was Socrates after all', BGE Preface, trans. Zimmern.

'The appearance of the Greek', WTP §427, 1887-88. 'Those moralists...who, following in the footsteps', D §9. 'Socrates [and thereby 'the mob']...achieved by means of', WTP §431, 1885-86; so too TI, 'The Problem of Socrates' §5. Thus 'the dialectical hero of the Platonic drama' (BT §14), 'Socrates for the first time recognized', EH on BT §1.

'I know of nothing more venomous', BGE §7; reported by Diogenes Laertius 10.8. Thus 'did Plato flee from reality', D §448. 'Plato is a coward', TI, 'What I Owe to the Ancients' §2.

p.25 P: 'the science of dialectic' (*Republic* 511) of eternal, perfect, Real Forms (ibid, 484-5); and the immortal soul Knows all these Essences before its rebirths (see Plato's, for example, *Phaedo* 72d-77a, 92c-d and *Meno* 81b-e). Plato claimed Forms of all worldly objects, excepting artistic creations (see Aristotle *Metaphysics* 1070a). All poetry is judged as poisonous without 'the antidote in a knowledge of its real nature' (*Republic* 595), and the imitative artist 'understands only the appearance, and not the reality' (ibid, 601). All dramatic compositions of the poets are 'phantoms' of imitation, 'twice removed' from real knowledge, that is, copies of representations of Forms (ibid, 599). Plato condemned drama as doubly deceptive imitation of illusion, to be banished from the ideal society (ibid, 393-9, 607), except for serious praises to the gods or virtue (ibid, 607); also banning the shrill pipes of the satyr Marsyas (ibid, 399). Quotes from *The Republic of Plato*, trans. Davies and Vaughan, 1852, MacMillan and Co., 1916 edition.

N: 'What did the Greeks admire', D §306.

P: 'tragedy and its leader, Homer', *Republic* 598 – 'there is a quarrel', ibid, 607 – 'the illusion of illusion', BT §4.

N: 'Plato versus Homer', GM, Third Essay §25.
'Plato...honoured and deified', WTP §431, 1888 – 'in the entire history of philosophy', WTP §460, 1888 – 'the most dangerous of errors...Good in Itself', BGE Preface, trans. Zimmern – as 'eternal treasure', WTP §972, 1884.

p.26 W: 'there is nothing which explains', LRB, II, p.63 – 'to call a proposition a 'picture''', Lectures 1930-33, reported by Moore, *Mind* volume LXIII, p.12. 'A *picture* held us captive', PI §115.

N: 'Oh how false', D 1886 Preface §3 – 'it is not true', TFUS.
'How I now regret', BT 1886 Preface §6; quoted on p.4.

p.27 'the expression of every deep', PTAG §3.'If he [man] does not mean to content himself', TFUS, greatly condensed text.

W: 'What is the meaning of a word?', opening BlB, 1933 – 'a picture...can be', PG §100, also *Zettel* §236 – 'sense...the life of the sign', BlB, p.4, 1933. 'Language is an instrument', PI §569 – 'the multiplicity of the tools', PI §23.

N: 'the insect and the bird', TFUS, condensed text.

W: 'There cannot be a question', PG §133; also PI, p.147 note.

p.28 'There really are cases', CV 1949. 'I never more than', CV 1931.

N: 'every creature different from us', WTP §565, 1886.

W: 'only of a living human being', PI §281.

N: 'tyrant...[of] conditions...imposed', WTP §354, 1888. 'Words are only symbols', PTAG §11 – 'past and future are as unreal', PTAG §5 – 'everything has evolved...nor...absolute Truths', HH §2, capital letter added for 'Truths', *Wahrheiten*.

p.29 W: 'our words will only express facts', 'A Lecture on Ethics', 17.11.1929, condensed text.
'misuse of our language runs through, 'A Lecture on Ethics', 17.11.1929, condensed text.
'humans will continue to bump', TBT §90, translated in *Philosophical Occasions*, p.424.
'Aesthetically, the miracle is', *Notebooks*, 20.10.1916; quoted on p.5 – 'the astonishment that anything exists', LWVC, 30.12.1929, trans. Murray 1967. 'No sign leads us beyond itself', PG §71; quoted on p.8. 'If you understand at all', Lectures 1930-32, Notes, p.114.
'Anything that I might reach', CV 6-7.11.1930 – 'a nothing would serve just as well', PI §304.

N: '*In prison*...I live', D §117 – 'a brazen wall of fate', AOM §33.

P: 'we therefore come up against', quoting from Schopenhauer: 'We cannot possibly escape...our intellect...we therefore come up against insoluble problems everywhere, as against the walls of our prison...For knowableness...belongs merely to the *phenomenon* ['representation'], not to the being-in-itself of things', *The World as Will and Representation*, volume II, §50, p.641.

p.30 N: 'we catch nothing at all except', D §§117-18.

       P: 'Life...as a fleeting...light', quoting from Schopenhauer: 'Life and its forms merely float before him [the saint] as a fleeting phenomenon [or 'appearance'], as a light morning dream to one half-awake, through which reality already shines and which can no longer deceive; and, like this morning dream, they too finally vanish', *The World as Will and Representation*, volume I, §68, pp.390-1.

Quoting Wagner's *Tristan and Isolde* (1859): 'Day's phantoms! Morning dreams' (Act II, Scene 3, Tristan). And finally Isolde: 'unconscious, supreme joy!' (*unbewusst, höchste Lust!*).

       N: 'the two most famous...*pessimism* ['dissatisfaction with reality', WTP §845, 1885-86]...music', GS §370 – 'weariness with life', 1886 Preface to AOM, §3 – 'that nerve-destroying music', letter to von Meysenbug, 1.7.1877, in SPL – 'Schopenhauer's scandalous misunderstanding', WTP §812, 1888. 'One summer at Bayreuth', letter to Maier, 15.7.1878, in SPL. 'I saw the great...seduction', GM Preface §5 – 'tragedy...of the sufferings', BGE §229.

'Schopenhauer's metaphysics...is false', letter to Fuchs, end of July 1877, in SPL – 'metaphysical befogging of everything', letter to Maier, 15.7.1878, in SPL – 'my great teacher Schopenhauer', GM Preface §5: 'he misunderstood genius, art', WTP §851, 1888 – 'he blundered in everything', EH on BT §1. 'Schopenhauer spoke of 'will'', WTP §95, 1887. 'Schopenhauer was hostile to life', AC §7.

       P: Wagner 'first came across' Schopenhauer's *Die Welt als Wille und Vorstellung* in 1854, and that book 'certainly exerted a decisive influence', Wagner's autobiography *My Life*, Constable 1911, 1994 edition, see pp.614-16. Wagner 'under the influence of Schopenhauer', ibid, p.731 –

p.31   'the serious mood created by Schopenhauer', ibid, p.617. It may be added here that Wagner also writes: in May 1857, 'I plunged anew into the philosophy of Schopenhauer' (ibid, p.659); and that summer 'I now prepared to write out Tristan' (ibid, p.667). 'I completed the composition of the whole work by the beginning of August [1859], fragments only remaining to be orchestrated' (ibid, p.711).

       N: '*Tristan*: it is a masterpiece', letter to Fuchs, 27.12.1888, in SPL. After receiving (on 3.1. 1878) a copy of Wagner's *Parsifal* 'poem' (the complete libretto; the music being composed over 1877-79, with the scored work finished in 1882), 'I went on alone', 1886 Preface to AOM, §3 – 'the [stage-] actor should not become', ending *The Wagner Case* essay, 1888 – 'not just mistaken, but *lying*', letter to von Salis, 14.11.1888, in SPL. '*in the "Birth of Tragedy"*...one encounters', WTP §853, draft for a Preface to BT, probably 1886, condensed text – 'nihilism ...[is] the belief', WTP §617, 1883-85. 'A nihilist...judges...the world', WTP §585, 1887-88.

p.32   'Richard Wagner...a despairing romantic', 1886 Preface to AOM, §3 – 'one should not let oneself', BGE §256. 'I am still grateful to him', letter to von Meysenbug, 14.1.1880, in SPL 'In individual moments we all know', UM III §5.

W: 'Our life is like a dream', letter to Engelmann, 9.4.1917.

N: 'If we had not welcomed the arts', GS §107.

W: 'it's strange that', *Philosophical Remarks* §47; also TBT §91. 'The ostensive definition', PG §45 – 'there is no confrontation', LWVC, 1.7.1932. 'Such words as 'and'', Lectures 1930-32, B IX, §2, 1931. 'The meaning of a proposition', 'Notes on Logic, 1913' – 'in no case is a word', Lectures 1930-33, reported by Moore, *Mind* volume LXIII, p.9.

'Grammar is not accountable to any reality', PG §133 –

p.33   'grammar...what makes it not arbitrary', Lectures 1930-32, B X, §5, 1931. 'What we call *"descriptions"*', PI §291.

N: 'as if there were an actual *drive*', WTP §423, 1888.

W: 'given a set of axioms', LFM, XXV.

N: 'How is truth proved?', WTP §455, 1888 – 'only certain truths are admitted', WTP §445, 1888.

W: 'Is it wrong for me to be guided', OC §§608-12. 'it has no meaning', OC §496. 'Whether a thing is a blunder', LRB, I, p.59 – 'rules can't collide, unless', PG §133, also partly in both PI, p.147 note and *Zettel* §320; quoted in part on p.27. 'If I change the rules', Lectures, 1930-32, A XI, §3, 1930. 'If I say: here we are', TBT §89, translated in *Philosophical Occasions*, p.183 – 'philosophy does not call on', TBT §86. 'Time and again the attempt is made', *Philosophical Remarks* §47; also TBT §91.

p.34 N: 'Language depends on', WTP §522, 1886-87.

W: 'aren't you neglecting something', PESD, pp.296-7. 'When I talk about language', PI §120. 'We are only interested', Lectures 1930-32, B IX, §2, 1931.

P: 'the philosophy of grey concepts', WTP §522, 1886-87.

N: 'Truth is ugly', WTP §822, 1888.

P: 'All that plurality, diversity', PTAG §10.

W: 'The solipsist flutters', PESD, p.300 – 'aim in philosophy', PI
§309 – of 'thoughts', PI §304, quoted more fully on p.72.
'Running against the limits', LWVC, 17.12.1930.
P: 'free thinking', letter to Rohde, 15.7.1882, in SPL.

Revaluation of Moral Ideals

p.35 N: 'We should not let ourselves', AOM §345.
'my "free thinking"', letter to von Salomé, 2.7.1882, in SPL – 'I
liberated myself', EH on HH §1 – 'human, all too human folly',
GS §374 – 'the daybreak of spiritual freedom', AOM §226 –
'lust for power', WS §6 – 'the will turning', GM Preface §5.
*'Twilight of the Idols (Götzen-Dämmerung), or: How to
Philosophize with a Hammer'* (that book's full title) – 'in plain
terms', EH on TI §1. 'To overthrow idols', EH Foreword §§2-4.
'I am herewith the *destroyer*', EH 'Why I am a Destiny' §2.
W: 'I was thinking about', CV 1931.
N: 'the good artist's', HH §155.
W: 'even the best poets', CV 1947.
'Where does our investigation', PI §118; the first two sentences
also in TBT §88.
N: 'building can be destroyed', AOM §201.
W: 'All that philosophy can do', TBT §88.
N: 'when man gets beyond superstitious', HH §20
p.36 – 'the end of metaphysical views', HH §22 – 'the old truth', EH
on TI §1, quoted on p.35.
W: 'Religious faith and superstition', CV 4.6.1948.
At the outbreak of war in 1914, when posted to Krakow, I
bought volume eight of your collected *Works* [editions usually
containing *Twilight of the Idols*, *The Anti-Christ*, *The Wagner
Case*, *Nietzsche contra Wagner* and Poems including *Dionysus-
Dithyrambs*]. I was 'very troubled' by your 'hostility to
Christianity' (*Diary* 8.12.1914). However, I had also found
Tolstoy's *Gospel in Brief*: and 'At this time, this book virtually
kept me alive' (letter to von Ficker, 24.7.1915).
N: 'the highest mountains', TSZ III 'The Wanderer'.
W: 'We have got on to slippery ice', PI §107.
N: 'longer duration of elevated feelings', GS §288 – 'the misty
valley below', AOM §237.
The following poem by Nietzsche, written in 1882 to his young
Russian lady-friend Lou von Salomé, evidently refers to the
previous year of his first summer in Sils-Maria, a village in the
Swiss Upper Engadine:

Hier sass ich, wartend, wartend, – doch auf nichts,
Jenseits von Gut und Böse, bald des Lichts
Geniessend, bald des Schattens, ganz nur Spiel,
Ganz See, ganz Mittage, ganz Zeit ohne Ziel.
Da, plözlich, Freundin! wurde eins zu zwei
– Und Zarathustra ging an mir vorbei...
(Quoted in German in *The Gay Science* Appendix.)

W: 'I summed up my attitude to philosophy', CV 1933-34 –
'*unpoetic* mentality', CV 5.11.1930. 'There are problems I never
get anywhere near', CV 1931.

p.37   N: 'Beethoven composed music above', AOM §171 condensed text.
W: 'Beethoven is a realist', *Diaries* 1.3.1931.
N: 'Around the hero', BGE §150.
'I know my fate', EH 'Why I am a Destiny' §§1-2; quoted in
part on p.1.
'I...understand myself as', EH on BT, §3.
'*I have been the first to discover*', WTP §1029, 1884-86 – 'life
can give no true satisfaction', BT 1886 Preface §6; quoting
Schopenhauer, *The World as Will and Representation*, volume
II, §37, pp.433-4.
'Dionysus is a philosopher', BGE §295; quoted on p.10.
P: 'the Dionysian procession', BT §20; quoted on p.3.

p.38   N: 'The tragedy begins', GS §342.
'Zarathustra was the first', EH, 'Why I am a Destiny' §3.
'my "free thinking"', letter to von Salomé, 2.7.1882, in SPL.
'When one has disclosed', HH §9 – '*noble* taste...[wise, calm
'victory' over and] above', EH on HH §1.
'we stand in need of a *critique*', GM Preface §6 – 'the *value* of
morality', ibid, §5. 'I see nobody who ventured', GS §345 –
'*alone*...I descended', D 1886 Preface §1 – 'the fundamental
insights', D §9, 1880-81.
'Strange madness of moral judgments!', D §189. 'Madness is
something', BGE §156 – 'supreme value...became master', WTP
§401, 1888 – 'human herds', BGE §199 – 'ideal of a shy', BGE
§212 – 'the herd-man', BGE §199.

p.39   'morality itself is a special case', WTP §401, 1888. 'Virtue is
our greatest misunderstanding', WTP §54, 1888. '"Virtue" made
completely abstract', WTP §428, 1888 – 'the serious illness',
GM Second Essay §16, trans. Hollingdale, condensed text –
'through...violence', ibid, §17, condensed text – 'the 'soul' first
develops', GM Second Essay §16.
'All human life is sunk', HH §34 – 'the spiritual and psychical
nature', WS §8. 'Man, imprisoned in...errors', WTP §397, 1888

– 'for thousands of years', HH §16.

'the saint, in whom the ego', UM III §5.

'their perpetual bitter resentment', UM III §3. 'You suffer...and *destroy*', D §214 – by 'asceticism...man takes a real delight', HH §137, trans. Hollingdale.

'Everything hitherto called 'truth'', EH 'Why I am a Destiny' §8. 'Almost everything we call 'higher culture'', BGE §229., partly quoted on p.30.

p.40 'Art is the great stimulus to life' TI, 'Expeditions of an Untimely Man' §24. 'One does not ['better'] understand', HH §29. 'The need for...revenge', WTP §376, 1883-88, trans, Hollingdale – 'this artistic cruelty', GM Second Essay §18 – 'artists...have raised to a heavenly transfiguration', HH §220. 'The artist...believes', HH §159 – '*will* in Schopenhauer's sense', BT §6. 'But now [I see] there is...art', GS §107.

'the cowardice of the 'idealist'', EH 'Why I am a Destiny' §3.

W: 'What I do think essential', CV 1931 – 'on the barren heights of cleverness', CV 1948.

N: 'Reality has been deprived of its value', EH Foreword §§2-4 condensed text.

W: 'One might say: 'Genius is'', CV 1940. 'Courage is always original', CV c.1939-40. 'Someone who does not lie', CV 1947.

N: 'I count nothing more', TSZ IV 'Of the Higher Man' §8.

W: 'Let me hold on to this', *Diaries* 13.2.1937.

N: 'our honesty, our will not to deceive', WTP §399, 1885-86 – 'honesty, compels us', WTP §404, 1886-87.

p.41 W: 'a man will never be great if', CV 1946.

N: 'One should not let oneself', AC §54.

W: 'Nothing is so difficult', CV 1938.

N: 'Honesty...is our [later: 'only'] virtue', BGE §226.

'*The free spirit (Freigeist)* [is] *a relative concept',* HH §225 – 'a series [of five books: HH, AOM, WS, D, GS]...whose common goal', from the back cover of GS – 'the *freedom*...our ideal', GS §107. 'I am...[an] immoralist', HH 1886 Preface §1.

'during the longest period', GS §117 – 'polytheism...in some distant overworld (*Überwelt*)...overmen (*Übermenschen*)...to oneself', GS §143 (Nietzsche's first mention of *Übermenschen*) – 'for will, as the affect of command', GS §347.

'Perhaps no one has ever', BGE §177. 'There has never yet been an *Übermensch*', TSZ II 'Of the Priests' – 'even the greatest all too human!', TSZ III 'The Convalescent' §2. *'Disgust* at mankind is my danger', EH 'Why I am a Destiny' §6 – 'go out especially to the song-birds, so that you may learn *singing* from them!', TSZ III 'The Convalescent' §2 – 'elevation, advance',

AC §4. By 'higher activity – I mean individual', HH §283.
'The discipline of...*great* suffering', BGE §225. 'The noble type
of man...*creates values*', BGE §260.
'the alchemist...changes', letter to Brandes, 23.5.1888, in SPL –
'alchemy in reverse', GS §292.

p.42 W: 'Man's greatest happiness is love', CV 1948.
N: 'one stops loving oneself', letter to Gast 18.7.1880.
'love acknowledges', HH §603. 'That which is done', BGE §153
– 'the whole concept of 'selfless action'', HH §133.
'My task...follows of necessity', EH on D §2.
'spiritual independence, the will', BGE §201. 'The free human
being is [called] immoral', D §9 – 'called criminals...bad men',
D §20 – 'the faith preached...that egoism', GS §328.
W: 'It's a good thing', CV 1929. 'Don't take the example', CV 1941.
N 'above the...human lowlands', WTP §993, 1885 – 'we...live on
mountains', GS §377.
'One should speak...only of', 1886 Preface to AOM, §1. 'I want
to hear your ruling idea', TSZ I 'Of the Way of the Creator'.

Nietzsche's Will to Power – to only Poetic Morality

p.43 N: 'explaining our entire instinctual life', BGE §36 – 'the cardinal
instinct', BGE §13, trans. Zimmern – 'the essence of life', GM
Second Essay §12– 'the really fundamental instinct', GS §349.
'All great things', GM Third Essay §27.
'To refrain from mutual injury', BGE §259 – 'life operates
essentially', GM Second Essay §11 – 'in real life', BGE §21.
'for will to come', GS §127. ''Willing' is not 'desiring'', WTP
§668, 1887-88. 'Willing liberates', TSZ III 'Of Old and New
Law-Tables' §16.
'in every act of will', BGE §19, trans. Zimmern – 'the
commander', TSZ II 'Of Self-Overcoming' – 'know morality as',
WS §45 – 'ever increasing elevation', AOM §99.
p.44 'this first outburst', HH 1886 Preface §3. 'It is not a matter',
WTP §358, 1887-88.
'But this loneliness', letter to von Meysenbug, 4.1884, in SPL –
'if I didn't sense', letter to von Meysenbug, 11.6.1878, in SPL.
'Am I a philosopher?', letter to Brandes, 10.4.1888, in SPL.
W: 'May it [my PI manuscript] soon', CV 1948 – 'from the bottom
of my heart', letter to Schlick, 8.8.1932.
N: 'spiritual freedom', WS §55 – 'a victory', AOM §152 – 'everyone
goes away...richer', BGE §295.
'Everyone has his good days', HH §624.

'my "free thinking"', letter to von Salomé, 2.7.1882, in SPL –
'the world is not good and not evil', HH §28 – 'good...beautiful
...evil...we impose', D §210 – 'men have given themselves',
TSZ I 'Of the Thousand and One Goals'.

W: 'What is good and evil', *Notebooks*, 5.8.1916; 'Good and evil
only enter', ibid, 2.8.1916; both quoted from p.9.

N: 'Thus the question', GS §344. 'In the great silence', D §423.
'You desire to *live*', BGE §9, trans. Zimmern – 'no longer like a
leaf', GM Third Essay §28.

p.45   'nothing is valuable "in itself"', WTP §260, 1883-88.
'To divide the world', TI, "Reason' in Philosophy' §6 – 'the
'real' world', ibid, §2 – 'the thing-in-itself', HH §16. The 'world
as idea', HH §19; so too §29. 'We have abolished', TI, 'How the
'Real World' at last Became a Myth' §6.

W: 'The meaning of a word', Lectures 1930-33, reported by Moore,
Mind volume LXIII, p.9.

N: 'the apparent *objective* character', WTP §560, 1887.
'the ascetic morality', WTP §388, 1887 – 'depersonalization of
the spirit', BGE §207 – 'the cult of "objectivity"', WTP §612,
1887. 'All experiences are moral', GS §114. '"Objectivity" in the
philosopher', WTP §425, 1887-88. 'It is the intellect's ambition',
AOM §156 – 'art "for its own sake"', WTP §29, 1883-88.
'Therefore: either no will', WTP §667, 1883-88 – 'science...
constitutes not the opposite', GM Third Essay §23 – 'knowledge
[means]...something familiar', GS §355.

W: 'is it...noticing for the first time', CV 5.11.1930.

N: 'belief in the ascetic ideal', GM Third Essay §24; similarly GS
§344. 'This unconditional will to truth', GS §344.

p.46   'Ultimately, man finds', WTP §606, 1885-86. 'Man first
implanted values', TSZ I 'Of the Thousand and One Goals'.
'In becoming everything is hollow', UM III §4 – 'perverse
wizards', HH §627 – in 'mysticism, the voluptuous enjoyment',
WTP §29, 1883-88 – like 'the teacher of', D §96.

P: 'the risk of longing' and 'yearning for the Void', BT §21, capital
letter added for 'Void', *Nichts*; quoted on p.10.
A detailed and fully referenced account of Buddhism is given
in *Oneself the Mystic and Philosopher*, Chapter 25, 'Siddhartha
Gautama: Buddha (No-)Dharma', pp.565-594. And a different
style of account of the Buddha's original teaching is given in
Jalendra and the Tathagata. More details of both these books
by the author follow at the end of this book.

N: 'The meaninglessness of suffering', GM Third Essay §28.

p.47   'reduce the physical world to an illusion', ibid, §12.
'willing directed by the ascetic ideal', ibid, §28 – 'human will...

must have a goal', ibid, §1. 'He who despises', BGE §78.
'the actual facts of the matter', GM Third Essay §13.
'Is meaning not necessarily relative', WTP §590, 1885-86 – 'life
itself is *determined*', HH 1886 Preface §6 – *'perspective* – the
fundamental condition', BGE Preface, trans. Zimmern. 'The
[individual's] will to power *interprets'*, WTP §643, 1885-86.
'Will to truth is a making firm', WTP §552, 1887.
'I consider *life itself instinct'*, AC §6.

p.48   'The higher human being...is really [or 'properly', *eigentliche*]
the poet', GS §301, 1881-82.
The 'sorcerer': 'I am banished from all truth, Only a fool! Only
a poet!', TSZ IV, ending 'The Song of Melancholy', 1883-85.
'Only a poet!...That must lie', *Dionysus-Dithyrambs*, 1888.
W: 'a poem, even though it is composed', *Zettel* §160.
N: 'We have *created* the world', WTP §602, 1884 – 'a 'free spirit'',
AC §32, 1888 – 'this life...poem', GS §301, 1881-82.

The Philosopher's Task of Twofold Necessity

p.49   N: 'Every word is a prejudice', WS §55 – 'a moral prejudice', BGE
§34 – 'every morality...is a protracted constraint', BGE §188.
W: 'Nothing is more difficult than', *Remarks on the Philosophy of
Psychology* II §12. 'One cannot guess', PI §340.
N: 'The will to power', WTP §656, 1887 – 'all expansion,
incorporation, growth', WTP §704, 1887-88.
W: 'Difficulty of philosophy [is] not the intellectual', TBT §86,
translated in *Philosophical Occasions*, p.161 – 'the conflict [or
'contrast', *Gegensatz*] between', TBT §86; also CV 1931.
N: 'philosophy is this tyrannical impulse', BGE §9, trans. Zimmern
– 'real [or 'proper', *eigentlicher*] *power*', BGE §252.
W: 'How small a thought it takes', CV 1946. 'In the [claimed]
theories', TBT §91, translated in *Philosophical Occasions*,
p.193 – 'we are dazzled by the ideal', PI §100.

p.50   'It is not in practical life', TBT §91. 'It is only in normal cases
that the use', PI §142.
'Philosophers are often like', TBT §91 and CV 1931 –
'"philosophy"...[is] the activity', Lectures 1932-35, 'Philosophy'
§23, 1932-33 – 'we are tempted', Lectures 1930-32, B 1931,
pp.60-61. 'The problems ['in philosophy'] are dissolved', TBT
§89, translated in *Philosophical Occasions*, p.183 – 'the
[arising] philosophical problems', PI §133; likewise TBT §89.
'in philosophy...our work', TBT §92; also *Zettel* §447.
'What *we* [philosophers need to] do', PI §116; so too TBT §88.

113

'It is not our aim to refine or complete', PI §133.

N: 'To employ innovations', WS §127.

W: 'What's ragged [or 'fuzzy', CV 1948] should be', CV c.1944.

N: 'Just as the good prose-writer', AOM §114.

W: 'In philosophy there is', TBT §89.

p.51 N: 'Their [philosophers' understanding or] thinking is', BGE §20, trans. Zimmern.

W: 'Learning philosophy really *is* a remembering', TBT §89. 'Grammar tells us what kind', PI §373. 'We remind ourselves... clearing ['the fog' (PI §5) of] misunderstandings away', PI §90.

N: 'metaphysics...might sound...befogging', BT, 1886 Preface §7. condensed text. 'Perspectival seeing is the *only* kind', GM Third Essay §12.

W: 'What has a soul', PI §283. 'Our attitude to', PI §284.

N: We 'have a *moral* origin', WTP §410, 1885-86 – 'led by instinctive moral definitions', WTP §407, 1884. 'Of decisive importance', WTP §258, 1885-86. 'To remain objective, hard', WTP §975, 1885-86. 'One seeks [to create] a...philosophy', WTP §418, 1883-88 – 'authentic instinct for life', GM Third Essay §12.

W: 'what is the use of studying philosophy', letter to Malcolm 16.11.1944.

N: 'faith in reason...is...moral', D 1886 Preface §4.

W: 'Philosophy unties knots',TBT §90, also *Zettel* §452 – such as of 'noun, adjective and verb', TBT §93.

N: 'the most valuable insights', WTP §469, 1888.

W: 'All I can give you is a method', Lectures 1932-35, Michaelmas term, X, p.97. 'I myself still find', CV c.1929.

p.52 'I know that my method is right', said to Drury in 1930, *Recollections of Wittgenstein*, ed. Rhees, OUP, 1984, p.110. 'confusion...considers', YB §17. 'We want to replace', TBT §92; also *Zettel* §447. '*Essence* is expressed by grammar', PI §371. 'The rules of grammar are independent', YB §14.

N: 'grammar (the metaphysics of the people)', GS §354.

W: 'the herd which has created', TBT §90 – 'the grammar of our ordinary language', LWVC, 9 12.1931.

N: "It is given", TSZ III 'Of the Virtue that Makes Small' §3 – 'to let oneself be determined',WTP §48, 1888.

W: 'the task of philosophy', PG §72.

N: 'The philosophical objective outlook', WTP §585, 1887-88.

W: 'Philosophy may in no way interfere', PI §124; also TBT §89.

N: 'creative positing...overcoming, willing', WTP §605, 1887.

W: 'philosophical problems...are solved [or 'dissolved', TBT §89;

quoted on p.50], not by', PI §109. 'Philosophy...neither explains nor deduces anything', PI §126; also TBT §89. Going 'through the thicket', CV 1949 – 'nothing is concealed', PI §435.

p.53   N: 'merely a believer', EH on TSZ §6 – 'where one did not know', D §40 – 'philosophers...must no longer accept concepts', WTP §409, 1885 – 'this task itself demands', BGE §211.

'Actual philosophers [the 'genuinely philosophical', BGE §213] ...are commanders', BGE §212 – 'they reach for the future', BGE §211. 'He who *determines* values', WTP §999, 1884 – through 'exercise of...the art of commanding', BGE §213.

new philosophers...[need to] teach man', BGE §203. 'Its meaning in four words', letter to Deussen, 14.9.1888, in SPL – 'the task of the philosopher dawns', WTP §422, 1885 – 'the future task of the philosopher', GM ending First Essay §17.

p.54   'The development of reason', WTP §515, 1888 – 'all life is based on appearance, art', BT 1886 Preface §5.

'The falseness of an opinion [or 'judgment'] is not for us any objection', BGE §4, trans. Zimmern.

'We sail straight over morality', BGE §23 – with 'a feeling of birdlike freedom', HH 1886 Preface §4. 'One must have liberated oneself', GS §380 – 'the abyss, the Spirit of Gravity', TSZ III 'Of the Vision and the Riddle' §§1-2.

'I would not know', GS §381 – 'intellectual *light feet*', TI, 'What the Germans Lack' §7. 'Only a poet...speaking colourfully', *Dionysus-Dithyrambs* 1888; quoted on p.48.

P: '*light* feet', TI, 'The Four Great Errors' §2.

N: 'What a philosopher is', BGE §213 – 'the real [or 'proper', *eigentlichen*] antithesis', EH on BT §2 – 'denial *and destruction*', EH 'Why I am a Destiny' §4.

'I contradict as has never', EH 'Why I am a Destiny' §§1-2. 'He contradicts with every word', EH on TSZ §6.

p.55   'My style is a dance', letter to Rohde, 22.2.1884, in SPL – 'thought...[is] a closest relation', BGE §213.

'I am suspicious [or 'mistrustful'] of dialectics', letter to Brandes, 2.12.1887, in SPL. 'The general imprecise', WS §67. 'What strange simplification', BGE §24.

W: 'my interest is in...*King Lear*: 'I'll teach you differences' [Shakespeare: Act I, Scene IV, line 99]', said to Drury in 1948, *Recollections of Wittgenstein*, ed. Rhees, OUP, 1984, p.157. "sense" is not "sharply bounded" – but means "a concept with blurred edges", quoted on p.22. 'Many words...don't have a strict meaning', quoted on p.22.

N: 'our *humanization* – a genuine', WTP §115, 1888 – 'shadow is as needful as light', WS Preamble.

Introspection as Essentially Defined

p.56   N: 'I am no seeker', GS §320. 'No, life has not disappointed', GS §324 – 'there exists a downright cult of suffering', BGE §293.

P: 'prison' of 'lies and deception', D §117.

N: 'we...deny the ['ascetic'] ideal', GM Third Essay §11, condensed text.
'psychology shall again be recognized', BGE §23.
'My life is now governed', letter to Overbeck, 2.7.1885, in SPL.
'I want to be right', letter to Deussen, 1886.

W: 'My investigation will not be psychological', YB §1.

N: 'the spell of definite', BGE §20. 'The body and physiology', WTP §492, 1885 – 'for what does one at present', BGE §10, trans. Zimmern – 'we *have* nothing but', WTP §574, 1883-88. 'sound method demands', GS §355.

p.57   'Life is...will to power', WTP §681, 1883-88 – 'the essential thing in the [organic] life process', WTP §647, 1883-88 – 'as will to power', WTP §617, 1883-85.
'In every judgment there resides', WTP §550, 1885-86. 'The separation of the 'deed'', WTP §631, 1885-86. 'But...there is no 'being' behind doing', GM First Essay §13.

W: 'The words 'soul' and 'mind', Lectures 1932-35, 'Philosophy' §28, 1932-33 – 'we then look for', YB §2.

N: ''Subject', 'object', 'attribute' [or 'predicate']', WTP §549, 1885 – 'the fictitious insertion', WTP §632, 1885-86. 'Subject, object, a doer', WTP §634, 1888 – 'it is only relations', WTP §625, 1888 – 'thingness has only', WTP §558, 1887.

W: 'what more can I do', PESD, p.297; quoted on p.34.

N: 'we see ourselves', TI "Reason' in Philosophy' §5.

W: 'Well, what would', reported by Anscombe. Wittgenstein once asked her: "'Why do people say that it was natural to think that the sun went round the earth rather than that the earth turned on its axis?" I replied: "I suppose, because it looked as if the sun went round the earth". "Well", he asked, "what would it have looked like if it had *looked* as if the earth turned on its axis?'" (*An Introduction to Wittgenstein's Tractatus*, Hutchinson University Library, 1959, p.151).

p.58   N: 'Language...*reason*...sees', TI "Reason' in Philosophy' §5 – 'the conception of...the ego', TI 'The Four Great Errors' §3 – 'our "ego" concept', WTP §635, 1888.

W: 'The word 'I' is one symbol', YB §11.

N: 'The *causa sui* is the best self-contradiction', BGE §21.
Some still 'believe 'immediate certainties' exist', BGE §16, trans. Hollingdale.

'thinking...invented the "ego"', WTP §574, 1883-88 – 'it is a *falsification*', BGE §17. "There is thinking", WTP §484, 1887.

W: 'It seems as though', PESD, pp.281-82 – 'to say...'I *am* in a favoured", ibid, pp.298-99 – or 'Descartes' emphasis', YB §11. 'Instead of saying 'I think", Lectures 1932-35, 'Philosophy' §§18-19, 1932-33.

p.59   '"I am..." Now in saying this', PI §404. 'I' is not the name of a person', PI §410 – "when anything is seen", BlB, p.63, 1934 – 'it is the particular use', BlB, p.69, 1934 – 'that it makes sense to suppose', YB §11. 'Does the solipsist also say', PESD, p.283.

N: 'the world is not an organism', WTP §711, 1887-88 – "nature's conformity to law", BGE §22. '"Regularity" in succession', WTP §632, 1885-86. '"Things" do not behave', WTP §634, 1888. 'The world...is...a fable', WTP §616, 1885-86. 'consciousness has developed only under', GS 354.

p.60   P: 'comparable, prison world of inescapable error [see D §117; quoted on p.29]...as for instance Socrates finally revealed', see GS §340; quoted on p.24.

N: 'The intellect cannot criticize itself', WTP §473, 1886-87. 'human intellect cannot avoid seeing itself', GS §374 – 'consciousness constitutes only one state', GS §357.

P: 'tyrant...[of] conditions', WTP §354, 1888; quoted on p.28.

N: 'The art of associating with people', GS §364. 'words dilute and brutalize', WTP §810, 1887 – 'to understand one another', BGE §268, trans. Zimmern. 'One has to get rid', BGE §43. 'A great man', WTP §962, 1885. 'Every superior human being', BGE §26.

p.61   'the continued existence of the rule', WTP §894, 1887. 'We no longer have', TI, 'Expeditions of an Untimely Man' §26 – 'in decay', BGE §203 – 'almost any word', BGE §22 – 'every metaphor of perception', TFUS.

W: 'Whereof one cannot speak...'? (beginning the last line of the *Tractatus*, quoted on p.15) – 'a nothing would serve', PI §304; quoted on p.29.

P: 'all life is dispute over taste and tasting!', TSZ II 'Of the Sublime Men'; quoted on p.3.

W: 'Every artist has been influenced by others', CV c.1932-34.

N: 'Unconsciously we seek out the principles', HH §608.

W: 'It is sometimes said that', CV 1931.

N: 'philosophical systems...all have', PTAG Preface, probably 1874. 'In the philosopher...there is', BGE §6. 'If the individual had not cared about', HH §634 – 'the *thinker's personal struggle*', HH §634.

p.62   'prejudiced...heart's desire', BGE §5, trans. Zimmern – 'spirit and taste', BT 1886 Preface §6 – 'creative positing', WTP §605, 1887, quoted on p.52 – [Nietzsche's Zarathustra:] 'not good taste...but *my* taste', TSZ III 'Of the Spirit of Gravity' §2.

W: ''taste' cannot create', CV 9.4.1947.
'we encounter philosophical problems', TBT §91; quoted on p.50 – 'it is the particular use', BIB, p.69; quoted on p.59.

N: 'Morality is...*practical*', WTP §423, 1888 – 'the practical sphere', WTP §579, 1883-88 – 'the practical interest', WTP §442, 1888.

P: Quoting Kant: 'theoretical philosophy (natural science)' and 'practical philosophy (ethical science)' (*Critique of Judgment*, Introduction I, 1790); that as moral or 'practical' concerns everything 'which *ought to be*', *Critique of Pure Reason* B 868. 'Act only according to that maxim...you can...will as universal law', *Foundations of the Metaphysic of Morals*, 1785, II, 421, trans. Beck, 1949 – 'the will of every rational being', ibid, 432.

p.63 N: 'unscientific basic', 1886 Preface to AOM §5 – 'all romantic', ibid, §3, part quoted on p.31 – 'to be a lawgiver', HH §261. 'I do not wish to promote', GS §292. 'I am a law only', TSZ IV 'The Last Supper' – 'first produce them', WTP §326, 1883-88. 'One should make one's own ideal', letter to von Meysenbug, August 1883, in SPL. 'This much is certain', letter to von Meysenbug, May 1884, in SPL. 'Whatever kind of', WTP §349, 1887-88. 'Let everyone be', letter to Maier, 15.7. 1878, in SPL – 'to experience one's own judgment', GS §335.

W: 'In what sense have you *got*', PI §398.

N: 'every action...[is] altogether unique', GS §335; likewise §120. '"Consciousness"...known to ourselves alone', WTP §476, 1884.

W: 'I know only indirectly what he', PESD, p.319.

N: 'my "free thinking"', letter to von Salomé, 2.7.1882, in SPL. 'The moral man...presumes', HH §4 1876 – 'the free spirit answers himself', HH Spring 1886 Preface §7.

W: 'If I say of myself', PI §293.

p.64 'The essential thing about private experience', PI §272. 'Always get rid of the idea', PI p.207.
'There is no subjective sureness that', OC §245. 'An inner experience cannot shew', OC §569.

N: 'the psychological derivation', WTP §473, 1886-87 – 'judgment is a belief', WTP §530, 1883-88.

W: 'a mental state of conviction', OC §42 – 'complete conviction, the total absence of doubt', OC §194.

N: 'The question of [moral] values', WTP §588, 1883-86.

W: 'What I know, I believe', OC §177. 'What is a telling ground', OC §271 – 'it needs to be *objectively* established', OC §15.

'"I know that" means', OC §16. 'One always forgets', OC §12.

'the elementary mistake', OC §397.

'If "I know etc." is conceived', OC §58.

'a telling ground', OC §271. 'There is therefore no occult act', Notes for 'Philosophy Lecture', possibly originally 1935-36, revised until 1942 – 'justification consists in appealing', PI §265 – '"sensation" is a word of our common language', PI §261. 'An 'inner process' stands in need', PI §580.

N: 'no *criterion of truth*', WTP §516, 1887-88; quoted on p.22.

W: 'What is the criterion for', LRB, II, p.62 – 'characteristic expression of pain', PI §142.

'it is sensible to ask', Lectures 1932-35, 'Philosophy' §16, 1932-33. '"I know where I am feeling pain"', OC §41.

N: 'nothing is 'given' as real except', BGE §36.

W: 'There is always the danger', OC §601.

N: 'the *erroneousness* of the world', BGE §34.

W: 'I need a criterion', PI §288. 'Are you not really', PI §307. 'What we deny', PI §305. 'Introspection can never lead', *Remarks on the Philosophy of Psychology*, volume I, p.212.

'If intuition is an inner voice', PI §213. 'A definition surely serves', PI §258; quoted on p.19 and p.22.

N: 'my feeling of *isolation*', letter to Overbeck, 5.8.1886, in SPL. 'I'm still just as alone', letter to Rohde, 11.11.1887, in SPL.

W: 'the way I have travelled', *Notebooks*, 15.10.16; compare T 5.64. 'In as much as it cannot be', PI §398. 'Don't concern yourself', CV 1947. 'The [unshareable] 'private experience' is a degenerate construction', PESD, p.314 – 'we only say that someone speaks', PI§ 344.

'Consciousness is as clear', *Zettel* §221.

Objective Practice and Subjective Interpretation

W: 'In order to describe the phenomenon', RFM, VI §34. 'The use of the word *in practice*', BlB, p.69, 1934.

N: '"to know"...[is] to impose upon chaos', WTP §515, 1888 – 'the practical interest', WTP §442, 1888; quoted on p.62.

W: 'Practice gives the words their sense', CV 1950.

N: 'There exists neither', WS §31. 'Rights can in the first instance', WS §39.

W: 'to communicate, people must agree', RFM, VI §39. 'If language is to be a means', PI §242; likewise RFM, VI §39.

N: 'That a great deal of *belief*', WTP §507, 1887.

W: 'a great deal of stage-setting', PI §257.

N: 'Believing is the primal beginning', WTP §506, 1884 – 'only in connection and relation', WTP §530, 1883-88.

W: 'learning is based on believing', OC §170 – 'we are taught *judgments*', OC §140-41.
'agreement decides what', PI §241.

N: 'This tree...if it', TSZ I 'Of the Tree on the Mountainside'.

W: 'If a lion could talk', PI, p.223.

p.68   'A symbol cannot by itself', Lectures 1930-32, B VI, §2, 1930.
'A word only has meaning', ibid, B V, §4, 1930 – 'the grammar of our ordinary language', LWVC, 9 12.1931, 'the herd which has created', TBT §90; both quoted on p.52.

N: "It is given", TSZ III 'Of the Virtue that Makes Small' §3; quoted on p.52. 'What is needed above all', WTP §409, 1885.

W: 'judgment...must begin with not-doubting', OC §150.
'a principle of speaking', OC §117. 'If you are not certain of any fact', OC §114. 'A doubt that doubted everything', OC §450.

N: 'it ['meaning'] is not a fact', BGE §22 condensed text.

W: 'one is not playing', OC §446. 'Doubt comes *after* belief', OC §160 – 'doubting itself presupposes certainty', OC §115 – 'we must commit ourselves', Lectures 1930-32, B V, §4, 1930.
'We must distinguish between a necessity', LFM, XXV; quoted on p.33. 'If I use a symbol', Lectures 1930-32, B VI, §2, 1930 – as "guided" or "led by language", Lectures 1930-33, reported by Moore, *Mind* volume LXIII, p.7. 'What is essential is that', Lectures 1930-32, B V, §4, 1930 – 'there must be rules', ibid, B X, §2, 1931 – 'what makes it ['grammar'] not arbitrary', ibid, B X, §5, 1931; quoted on p.33.

N: 'Trust in reason...proves only', WTP §507, 1887. 'What "useful" means is entirely dependent', WTP §724, 1887.

W: '"measuring" is partly determined', PI §242 – 'the result is part of the technique', LFM, VIII.

p.69   N: 'with different intentions', BGE §22, trans. Zimmern – '"reality" is always only simplification', WTP §580, 1887 – '"knowing" intellect encounters a coarse', WTP §520, 1885.

W: 'it is easy to get into that dead-end', PI §436.

N: 'the [scientist's] mechanistic interpretation', WTP §618, 1885.

W: 'It was true to say', PI §109; quoted on p.16. 'Our method is *purely descriptive*', BrB, p.125.

N: '"Interpretation", the introduction of [subjective] meaning', WTP §604, 1885-86 – 'everything of which we', WTP §477, 1887-88 – 'there is...only interpretations', WTP §481, 1883-88.

W: 'a principle of speaking', OC §117; quoted on p.68.

N: 'Necessity is not a fact', WTP §552, 1887.
'my "free thinking"', letter to von Salomé, 2.7.1882, in SPL –

'truths...they still appear to us', D §460, 1880-81. 'Granted this too is only interpretation', BGE §22.

p.70 W: 'if I am dreaming', OC §38.
'a symbol – which can be reinterpreted', LFM, XIX. '"Whatever I do is, on some interpretation"', PI §198.
N: 'supposing that a philosopher has always', BGE §289.
W: 'If I have exhausted the justifications', PI §217 – 'my reasons will soon give out', PI §211.
'This was our paradox: no course of action', PI §§201-2.

p.71 N: 'To submit, to follow', D §207 – 'all becoming conscious involves', GS §354; quoted on p.59. '"Regularity" in succession is only', WTP §632 1885-86; quoted on p. 59.
P: 'the commander...must...practice', TSZ II 'Of Self-Overcoming'; quoted on p.43.
N: 'that you take this or that judgment', GS §335.
W: 'When I obey a rule', PI §219.
N: 'Rights can in the first instance', WS §39; quoted on p.67.
W: 'One does not learn to', RFM, V §§32-33. 'What I do [in 'the beginning'] is not, of course', PI §290. 'To use a word without a justification', PI §289.
'A rule is best described as', Lectures 1932-35, XIII 1934-35, p.155.
N: 'the spirit is...as much at home', WTP §1051, 1885. 'We want to hold fast to our senses', WTP 1046, 1884.

p.72 W: 'it has no meaning to say', OC §496; quoted on p.33.
N: 'the *sense for facts*', AC §59. Now 'our attitude toward art', WTP §120, 1887. 'One should not conceal and corrupt', WTP §424, 1885. 'Error is *cowardice*', WTP §1041, 1888; see also EH Foreword §§2-4, quoted on p.40.
W: 'Courage is always original', CV c.1939-40, and 'who does not lie', CV 1947; both quoted on p.40.
P: 'Scientific philosophy' (HH §131; quoted on p.16) of 'cleansing knowledge' (HH §34), of 'imported' (WTP §606, 1885-86; quoted on p,46).
N: 'a 'free spirit'...cares nothing', AC §32, 1888; quoted on p.48.
P: 'the cult of "objectivity"', WTP §612, 1887 – the philosopher's "knowing' is *creating*', BGE §211.
W: 'we make a radical break', PI §304.
P: 'we do not permit ourselves any bridges-of-lies', D 1886 Preface §4; quoted more fully on p.78.
'reduce the physical world', GM Third Essay §12; quoted more fully on p.47 – 'this...*hostility to life*', BT 1886 Preface §5; quoted on p.12.

p.73 'the [every-day] requirements of the individual', WS §6; and 'we too have inherited something', WS §16 – 'incomprehensible, elusive', WTP §604, 1885-86, quoted on p.69 – 'you yourself' vengefully 'destroy', D §214; quoted more fully on p.39.

N: 'between two utterly different spheres', TFUS; quoted on p.27. 'Actions are never what they appear', D §116 – 'every action... [is] altogether unique', GS §335; quoted on p.63.

Language-games

p.74 W: 'I used to believe that', LWVC, 12.1929. 'It is *primarily* the apparatus', PI §494. We need 'to have a clear view...of what the ideal [or 'model', PI §131] is', CV 1937; likewise PI §131 – 'a preconceived idea ['of crystalline purity', PI §108] to which reality *must* correspond', PI §131.

N: 'to be a lawgiver', HH §261, quoted on p.63 – 'oppressing... excessive claims', HH §137 quoted on p.39.

W: 'The first step is the one', PI §308.

N: 'that master expedient', AOM §98.

W: 'We see that what we call', PI §108. 'At the root of all this', PG Appendix 4B, probably 1936 addition; first line quoted on p.17 – 'these phenomena have no one thing', PI §65. 'We shall compare the use', YB §3.

N: 'What strange simplification', BGE §24. quoted on p.55 – 'science itself *requires*', GM Third Essay §24, quoted on p.45.

W: 'one learns the meaning', RFM, V §§32-33, quoted on p.71 – 'for an explanation', TBT §89, translated in *Philosophical Occasions*, p.177 – "further descriptions", Lectures 1930-33, reported by Moore, *Mind* volume LXIV, p.19.

p.75   'Nothing we do', CV 13.9.1931, p.23. 'In certain circumstances', OC §212.
'a language-game is only possible', OC §509 – 'we have to... *accept* the everyday', PI, p.200.
'The the end [of 'giving grounds'] is not', OC §110. 'Giving grounds...justifying the evidence', OC §204. 'Sure evidence is what we *accept*', OC §196. 'To know its meaning', LFM, XIX; similarly *Zettel* §309.
'in philosophical investigation: the difficulty', *Zettel* §314. 'Words are also deeds', PI §546, likewise CV c.1945 – 'and write with confidence "In the beginning was the deed"', OC §402, also CV 1937, quoting Goethe, *Faust* 1.3, line 1237. 'Is our confidence justified?', PI §325.

N: 'if ever I have laughed with', TSZ III 'The Seven Seals' §3. 'Believing is the primal', WTP §506, 1884; quoted on p.67.

p.76   'philosophers...traverse the whole range', BGE §212.

W: 'the task of philosophy', PG §72; quoted on p.52.

'How hard I find it to see', CV 1940 – 'one...becomes aware of the most', *Diaries* 1930; quoted in *Ludwig Wittgenstein: Public and Private Occasions*, p.11. 'The solution of philosophical problems', CV 1931 – 'philosophical...answers will only be correct', TBT §88.

N: 'idealists of every description', WS §6; in part quoted on p.73.

W: 'Now what makes it difficult', BlB, pp.17-18, 1933. 'Not only rules, but also examples', OC §139. 'The words "non-sense" and "sense" get their meaning', Lectures 1932-35, 'Philosophy' §17, 1932-33 – sense is 'without a *fixed* meaning', PI §79.

'what I call 'language games'', Lectures 1932-35, XI, 1934-35, p.101 – 'these games are complete', Lectures 1932-35, 'Philosophy' §11, 1932-33.

'I have explained [or rather described]...a proposition', YB §15. 'I am giving grammatical examples, TBT §90. 'Propositions do not all', YB §15.

'Now I think of the meanings as like fibres', 29.7.1941, reported by Thouless, quoted in *Ludwig Wittgenstein: Public and Private Occasions*, p.387. 'A rope...is not of *one* piece', from a discussion in November 1944, ibid, p.363 – 'a rope...consists of fibres', BrB, p.87, 1934; likewise PI §67.

p.77   'We are inclined to think that', BlB p.17, 1933. 'Consider for example the proceedings', PI §§66-67 condensed text.

N: Philosophers' 'thinking is...a remembering', BGE §20, trans. Zimmern; in part quoted on p.51.

Religious Language

p.78 N: 'The madman...cried incessantly', GS §125. My 'Zarathustra... is merely an old atheist', WTP §1038, 1888. 'Zarathustra the Godless!', TSZ III 'Of the Virtue that Makes Small' §3 – 'this God which I created', TSZ I 'Of the Afterworldsmen'. 'All gods are dead', TSZ I 'Of the Bestowing Virtue' §3.

W: 'Religion as madness is a madness', CV 1931.

N: 'religions are affairs of the rabble', EH 'Why I am a Destiny' §1 – 'there is no God', AOM §225. 'God...belongs to the realm of fable', HH §133.

'God is dead; but...we still have to vanquish', GS §108. 'Let us beware of thinking that', GS §109.

'we who are godless', GS §280 – 'do not permit [ourselves] any ultimate (or 'final', *letzten*) Wisdom (*Weisheit*)...Goodness

(*Güte*)...Power (*Macht*)...Peace (*Freiden*)', GS §285, four capitals added – 'we do not permit ourselves any...Ideals... Idealism', D 1886 Preface §4, capital letters added for 'Ideals', *Idealen*, and 'Idealism', *Idealismus*, in part quoted on p.72 – 'higher...man...is looking down', HH §280.

'we find that which has been reverenced', AC §47 – '*lies* from the bad instincts...'God', 'soul', ['spirit', 'free will', EH on D §2] 'virtue'', EH 'Why I Am So Clever' §10.

'religions [are] for *sufferers*', BGE §62, trans. Zimmern.

W: 'People are religious to the extent', CV c.1944, 1998 edition.

P: 'Socrates finally revealed', see GS §340; quoted on p.24.

p.79 N: 'a divinity that sacrifices itself', HH §138 – 'those who suffer', GS §370 – 'lack of personality', GS §345 – 'what? is love supposed to', D §145. 'One has to be set firmly', EH 'Why I Write Such Good Books' §5.

W: 'Man's greatest happiness is love', CV 1948; quoted on p.42.

N: 'The priest knows only *one* great danger', AC §49 – 'the whole religio-moral interpretation', WTP §1019, 1887-88.

'the triumph of scientific atheism', GS §357 – 'the lie of belief in God', GM Third Essay §27.

'The ungodliness of existence', GS §357.

W: 'Schopenhauer is quite a crude mind', CV c.1939-40.

N: ''The father' in God is thoroughly refuted', BGE §53.

W: 'If the question arises', LRB, I, p.59.

N: ''Faith' means not *wanting* to know', AC §52. 'What thinking person still needs', HH §28.

W: For 'religious belief...different words', LRB, I, pp.56-57.

p.80 'My attitude towards him', PI, p.178.

'In a religious discourse we use such expressions' – as 'belief', 'experience' and 'evidence' – 'entirely differently' compared to 'ordinary' or 'scientific' language, LRB, I, pp.57-58. 'The point is that if there were evidence', LRB, I, p.56.

'Religious faith and superstition', CV 4.6.1948; quoted on p.36.

N: 'Convictions are more dangerous', HH §483. What 'has made history so violent', HH §630 – 'intense feeling, which guarantees nothing', HH §15 – 'what first led to the positing', GS §151. 'Conviction is the belief that...absolute [or "unconditional"] Truth', HH §630, capital letter added for 'Truth', *unbedingten Wahrheit*.

W: A man's personal need to pray 'is just what he does', *Diaries* 20.2.1937. 'Call it a sickness!', *Diaries* 19.2.1937.

'I can't contradict that person', LRB. I, p.55.

p.81 'you can call it believing the opposite', LRB, I, p.55 – 'this [religious] belief does not rest on', LRB, I, p.54.

'In religion talking is not metaphorical', LWVC, 17.12.1930.
Religious 'expressions...are not similes', *Diaries* 15.2.1937.
'this proves nothing for or against the Absolute (*das Absolute*)
...the Absolute (*das Absolute*)', letter to Hänsel, 9.2.1937, in
Ludwig Wittgenstein: Public and Private Occasions, p.293,
capital letter added twice for 'Absolute'.

N: 'the worst of all tastes...the Unconditional (*Unbedingte*)', BGE
§31, capital letter added for 'Unconditional' – 'everything
Unconditional (*Unbedingte*) belongs in pathology, BGE §154,
capital letter added for 'Unconditional'.

W: 'I wouldn't call them', LRB, I, pp.58-59, condensed text.

N: "'I believe because it is absurd"', HH §630.

W: 'Don't for heaven's sake', CV 1947.
In religion it 'does not matter at all', LWVC, 17.12.1930 – 'the
words you utter', CV 1950 – 'unshakeable belief...will show',
LRB, I; quoted on p.11.
'I have no faith...Let's cut out the transcendental twaddle [or
'babble', 'idle chatter'] when the whole thing is as plain as a
sock on the jaw (*Nur kein transzendentales Geschwätz, wenn
alles so klar ist wie eine Watschen*)', letter to Engelmann
6.1.1918; and again wrote to him, 'I have no faith', 21.6.1920.

p.82   'Yes I do, but the difference', from 1944; quoted by Rhees to
Monk in the latter's biography *Ludwig Wittgenstein*, p.463.
'Suppose someone said: "What do you believe"', LRB, III, p.70.
'God does not reveal himself in the world', T 6.432.

P: Gospels quoting Jesus, 'Son of man': "Render unto Caesar",
Mark 12.17, Luke 20.25, Matthew 22.21 – "and give Me what
is mine", added in Thomas 100.

N: 'Life should be ordered on the basis', WS §320.
'The worst thing is', BGE §53 – 'the divine privilege', D §544.
Epicurus called the Platonists deceitful Dionysian actors, BGE
§7, quoted on p.24 – 'as hatred of *every* reality...into the
'inconceivable' (*Unbegreifliche*), as antipathy', AC §29.

W: 'a religious belief could only be', CV 1947.
'The problems of life', CV 1948.

p.83   'What gives it ['engulfed' religious thought] depth', *Diaries*
1.12.1936.

N: 'The man of faith', AC §54. 'Faith in oneself', GS §284 – 'one
could conceive of such', GS §347.

W: 'An honest (*ehrliche*) religious thinker', CV 1948.
'skill at playing the game', CV 1937.

N: 'When one has disclosed', HH §9; quoted on p.38. 'God is
thoroughly refuted', BGE §53; quoted on p.79 – '*noble*
['victory']...above...this *underworld*', EH on HH §1, 1888.

P: 'It is not true, as prejudice', D §108.

N: "higher' and 'lower'...no absolute Morality', D §139, capital letter added for 'Morality', *Moral*.

'we cannot reject the possibility', GS §374.

p.84 W: 'Interpretations by themselves', PI §198; quoted on p.70.

P: 'to be a lawgiver', HH §261; quoted on p.63 and p.74.

'interpretation...assuming that it is not a mental illness', GS §373 – 'perhaps a pathological state', GS §357; quoted on p.60.

N: 'an essentially mechanistic world', GS §373.

W: 'to follow a musical phrase with understanding', CV 1946.

'This is where religion and art part', CV 5.11.1930.

N: 'at the basis of every religion', TI 'The Four Great Errors' §2.

W: 'Rules of [personal] life...can only serve', CV 24.9.1937.

'an ethical proposition is a personal act', *Diaries* 6.5.1931.

N: 'knowledge would be in a bad way', D §459.

W: 'subjective...[and] objective...betoken', PI p.225. 'Look on the language-game as the *primary* thing', PI §656.

Eternal Recurrence

p.85 N: In poetic '*inspiration*...a thought flashes up', EH on TSZ §3 condensed text – 'great admiration for [the ability]...to say', AOM §219, 1878 – 'no trace of *struggle* can be discovered in my life', EH 'Why I Am So Clever' §9, 1888.

W: 'is it possible for one', *Notebooks*, 6.7.1916; quoted on p.21.

N: 'The great confusion', WTP §703, 1888. 'I do not exhort you to peace', TSZ I 'Of War and Warriors', p.74 – 'a victory – an overcoming', AOM §152; quoted on p.44.

'painful compelled conformity and constraint', BGE §213 – 'to see as beautiful', GS §276.

'To remain objective...in carrying through', WTP §975, 1885-86; quoted on p.51 – 'greatness in a human being is *amor fati*', EH 'Why I Am So Clever' §10.

P: 'eternal recurrence': this idea first came to Nietzsche amidst the Swiss alpine region in August 1881 (see EH on TSZ §1), when he also mentioned Zarathustra and 'beyond good and evil' in the poem 'Sils-Maria', quoted on p.36.

p.86 N: 'the idea of eternal recurrence [is] the highest', EH on TSZ §1: 'What, if..."This life...you will have to live"', GS §341.

'I, the teacher of the eternal recurrence', TI 'What I Owe to the Ancients' §5 – 'wish' of the future higher person: 'you resist any ultimate peace', GS §285 – 'beyond good and evil, and no longer', BGE §56.

'The doctrine of 'eternal recurrence'', EH on BT §3.
'the Pythagoreans...believing that when', UM II §2.

P: Quoting Heraclitus: it is Zeus' 'thunderbolt' that 'steers all';
'conflict [or 'strife', *eris*] is justice' through which inescapable
necessity 'all things come to pass', as administered by the
Furies (fragments 64, 41, 80, 94 - Diels & Kranz) – 'turnings of
fire' (fragment 31 - Diels & Kranz).

N: 'Heraclitus will always be right in this', TI, "'Reason' in
Philosophy' §2. 'Heraclitus: we cannot step into the same river
twice. – This is...as true', AOM §223.

p.87 W: 'The man who said that one cannot step', TBT §88, translated in
Philosophical Occasions, p.167. 'The truly apocalyptic view',
CV 1947. 'In order to describe the phenomenon', RFM, VI §34;
quoted on p.67.

N: 'He who has attained to only some', HH §638, final paragraph
– 'we...instinctively attribute a deeper', GS §357.
'Becoming as invention', WTP §617, 1883-85 – 'all actions are
essentially unknown', D §116; quoted on p.73.
'must we not all', TSZ III 'Of the Vision and the Riddle' §2 –
'causes of the eternal recurrence', TSZ III 'The Convalescent'
§2 – 'the Ring of Recurrence', TSZ III 'The Seven Seals' §1.
'That everything recurs', WTP §617, 1883-85. 'This world...
[is] a sea of forces', WTP §1067, 1885.

P: 'able *to be different*', WTP §358, 1887-88; quoted on p.44.

N: 'to interpret and inflate', 1886 Preface to AOM §5; quoted on
p.63 – 'to experience one's own judgment', GS §335; quoted
on p.63 – 'inflated, oppressive art', 1886 Preface to AOM §3;
quoted on p.63.

p.88 W: 'all facts are contingent', Lectures 1930-32, C XIII,1931-32,
p.93; quoted on p.14.
'The freedom of the will consists in', T 5.1362.

N: 'Joy...wants eternity', TSZ IV 'The Intoxicated Song' §9.

Epilogue

p.89 N: 'With *Ecce Homo*', letter to Fuchs, 27.12.1888, in SPL.

W: "further descriptions", Lectures 1930-33, reported by Moore,
Mind volume LXIV, p.19; quoted on p.74.

N: 'Am I a philosopher? Who cares?', letter to Brandes, 10.4.1888,
in SPL; quoted on p.44. 'I...understand myself as the first
tragic philosopher', EH on BT §3, quoted on p.37 – 'my new
philosophy', letter to von Meysenbug, 11.6.1878, in SPL,
quoted on p.44. 'One seeks a...philosophy', WTP §418, 1883-

88; quoted on p.51 – 'real [or 'proper', *eigentlicher*] *power* of spirituality', BGE §252, quoted on p.49 – 'philosophers... traverse the whole range', BGE §212, quoted on p.76 – 'a philosophy...has thereby alone', BGE §4, trans. Zimmern, quoted on p.54 – '*new philosophers*...[need to] teach...a revaluation of values', BGE §203, quoted on p.53 – 'the future task of the philosopher', GM ending First Essay §17.

W: 'Practice gives the words their sense', CV 1950, quoted on p.67 – 'it is the particular use', BlB, p.69; in part quoted on p.59, p.62 and p.67.

N: 'being fair...demands much practice', D §112 – 'the only possible right way', HH §203.

p.90   W: 'a consensus of action', LFM, XIX, similarly *Zettel* §309; quoted on p.75.

P: 'only interpretation', BGE §22, quoted on p.68 and p.69; likewise WTP §481, 1883-88, quoted on p.69.

W: 'Nothing is more important for teaching', CV 1948 – 'to remove some trouble caused...our method is not merely to enumerate actual usages', BlB, p.28, 1933; quoted in part on p.22.

p.91   'I realized...The best that I could write', PI Preface, 1945. 'It is difficult to paint an adequate picture', CV 1949.
'My main movement of thought is a completely', *Diaries* 28.1.1932. 'It suddenly seemed to me that I should publish those', PI Preface, 1945. 'I should not like my writing to spare', PI Preface, 1945.
"obeying a rule' is a practice', PI §202; quoted on p.70.

Details of four further books by the author

From the back cover of the book:

ONESELF
THE MYSTIC
AND PHILOSOPHER

So much in the recognition and development of different conceptual kinds of understanding, that is, the philosophy of linguistic practices, consists in presenting clarification of the work of others. This book contains many quotations from influential great figures, calling out across the decades and centuries, to engage as directly as possible in detailed 'dialogues' – most extensively here with Ludwig Wittgenstein and Friedrich Nietzsche, undeniably two of the greatest philosophers ever. Correct and inspirational philosophy finds a clear expression in accepting, or making more explicit, their insights: that is, the later Wittgenstein's trailblazing clarification of objective certainty of given 'language-games', together with Nietzsche's explosive moral re-evaluation from a perspective of 'interpretation' as well as poetic creativity. Developed in such a way, the courageously profound writings of these two men, expressing different emphasis, complement each other wonderfully. Relative freedom to will any meaning so called essentially involves objective concept creation; any participant in such practice must combine descriptive conceptual rules with personal moral choices. This book divides into three parts:

PART I

The first two chapters, entitled 'Philosophical Descriptions' and 'Twilight of the Ascetic Idealists', engage with and develop upon some main insights of Wittgenstein and Nietzsche. It is accordingly recognized, against an enormous amount of most imaginative yet unrealizable idealism, that correct philosophy is always objective unjustifiable conceptual description – itself never science, yet only illustratively known in practice – and that any claim to absolutely complete selflessness is harmful conceptual blunder of the ascetic vengefully turned against life.

PART II

The bulk of this book provides a select detailed critical study of the works of highly influential Western philosophers, in chronological order: from the very first ancient Greek philosophers to Pythagoras, Heraclitus, Parmenides, some fifth century contemporaries, with Socrates calling for moral self-examination followed by Plato imagining Forms. A leap is then made to more modern Western philosophy: from its so-called 'founding' thought of Descartes, to Kant's 'Pure Reason' and Schopenhauer's World of Illusion. Nietzsche and Wittgenstein in their youth each fell deeply under the spell of Schopenhauer's unrealizable idealism, that itself draws upon Indian mysticism. The in-depth account given here of Nietzsche's writings extends from *The Birth of Tragedy* to a critique of his 'perspectival interpretation'. Next, the logical works of Frege and Russell, discussed briefly, also captivated the early Wittgenstein. The in-depth account of Wittgenstein's philosophy extends from his early to the later periods, that is, from ideal 'pictures' of the *Tractatus*, lasting even in transition, until their eventual complete replacement with recognition of radically different 'language-games'; and this account traces the development of his conception of philosophy.

PART III

The final 101 pages of this book aim to articulate conceptual sense, or senselessness, of the mystic and scripture, that is, 'Philosophical Spirit', focusing on the statements of three 'individuals': Siddhartha Gautama 'Buddha (No-)Dharma', sayings of Jesus 'Son of man', and also Ramana Maharshi 'Self-Enquiry'. Recognition of any statement made thereby shows acceptance of some objective practice, that is, definition of its relative terms as conceptually known. Personal statement is always relatively objectively defined yet otherwise unaccountable to science (known evidence). The ascetic's so-called complete selflessness is complete falsity, lacking any genuine compassion or wisdom in deed. The personal as such, including any aesthetic or moral judgment and religious belief (making sense or senseless), remains the entitlement of any individual embodied spirit.

'Contents' page from the book:
ONESELF
THE MYSTIC
AND PHILOSOPHER

This book *Oneself the Mystic and Philosopher* by Tony Hosking
(642 pages, 2014) ISBN 978 09531 08954
is available from its publisher: shogifoundation.co.uk

From the back cover of the book:

VISHNU-KRISHNA
SHIVA-SHAKTI

This book provides a select detailed critical study of Indian scripture and ritual practice, from ancient Vedas to more modern diverse Tantra, to clarify sense or senselessness and moral judgment of the devotee and mystic. Vedic violent, blood-stained, sacrificial killings would become widely replaced by the Upanishads proclaiming mystical Oneness, and from Epic times by expression of personal belief in the Lord, especially Vishnu or Shiva. Subjects in the account offered here include:

*   Brief remarks on the Indus Valley civilization.
*   An outline of sources and dating of Hindu scripture.
*   Introduction to early Indian Vedic Era c.1700-c.700 BC: pantheon, ritual sacrifices centring on the threefold Mouth as Agni (god of fire), Soma (god of the intoxicating drink) and Vac (goddess of chanting).
*   Rudra as first feared outsider (*asura* excluded from sacrifice), then 'Lord of animals' (*pashupati*) and 'auspicious' (*shiva*) healer.
*   Development of belief in karmic rebirths or 'long' immortality.
*   Upanishads affirming *brahman* One Self (*atman*) and Self-enquiry.
*   Cults c.5th century BC: Jains and Buddhists, Samkhya and Yoga.
*   Krishna's *Bhagavad Gita* teaching 'selfless Self-Knowledge'.
*   Epic ascent of Vishnu and Shiva: through the *Mahabharata*, *Ramayana*, Daksha's sacrifice, devotion (*bhakti*) and Shiva *linga*.
*   Goddess (*devi*) becoming Supreme: Shri-Lakshmi, sacrifice by Daksha then of Sati - reborn as Parvati - and the *Devi Mahatmyam*.
*   Symbolism of the rise of Shiva dancing (Nataraja).
*   Tantric cosmic and subtle chakras, *kundalini* and Kali.

Religious practice essentially expresses concepts and moral choices. The critical remarks given are primarily inspired by the insights of two men: Nietzsche's moral re-evaluation of 'only interpretation' combined with Wittgenstein later clarifying objective definition of religion. Contra so much unrealizable idealism, correct philosophy means only objective unjustifiable conceptual description; and the ascetic's total 'selflessness' is falsity turned against life. Religious belief is always relatively defined and personal entitlement of any embodied spirit. The final concepts, on tragic compassionate wisdom, express individual freedom of necessity – drawing upon *Oneself the Mystic and Philosopher*.

This book *Vishnu-Krishna Shiva-Shakti*
by Tony Hosking (189 pages, 2018) ISBN 978 09531 08978
is available from its publisher: shogifoundation.co.uk

From the back cover of the book:

JALENDRA AND THE TATHAGATA

This book aims to make clear sense, or senselessness, of the teaching (*dharma*) given by Siddhartha Gautama, called the 'selfless' Tathāgata ('Thus-gone') or Buddha ('Awakened').

The story related here is set just a few days after Gautama sat under the *bodhi* tree and 'attained' selfless Enlightenment, before teaching the first group of ascetics in Kashi (Varanasi). Walking there, the Tathagata is ferried by Jalendra across river Ganga. Jalendra talks of being guided by compassionate wisdom of goddess Ganga. The Tathagata proclaims having renounced all in Noble Knowledge. Then they sit in the shade of a quiet grove beside the river, and the Tathagata conveys the *dharma* of selfless Freedom from suffering the bondage of Ignorance, that is the universal causally Fated Wheel of actions (*karma*) and rebirth – all now Known as unreal, empty appearance. Jalendra is astounded, fascinated, but also deeply perplexed. Together they undertake self-seeking within.

Jalendra leaves to visit his beloved, beautiful Kamini. The two young companions enjoy their quite simple village life beside Ganga, yet they have also gained some understanding of priestly and ascetic teachings at the temples. Jalendra tells her about the *dharma*, which they discuss.

Returning to talk with the Tathagata, Jalendra emphasizes accepted public certainty defines any statement made, including the *dharma*, as recognized by someone; and any personal belief is defined entitlement of embodied spirit. But the Tathagata now proclaims *nirvana*, universal extinction: no self, no thing and finally no *dharma*. Jalendra affirms real compassionate wisdom is through individual freedom from unreal Fate. The Tathagata, as seemingly destined, walks on towards Kashi up river, thus gone; and as the sun sets, Jalendra floats in his little boat, choosing to steer east, trusting, joyfully borne by ever-flowing goddess Ganga.

The brief Epilogue is on Hesse's *Siddhartha*: a novel written in very fine poetic style, but his impossibly romantic tale mistakenly obscures the Buddha's *dharma*, claiming there is no better teaching.

The *dharma* admits, having appeared to dispel all as dark ignorance, it too must be mistaken and abandoned – there is no universal selfless emptiness! – but it gives totally wrong reasons, even causes for this dual (conceptual and moral) necessity. *Jalendra and the Tathagata* lifts the twofold false veil, sets the record straight, by some correct conceptual descriptions making clear, exposing the real philosophy of Buddhism.

This book *Jalendra and the Tathagata* by Tony Hosking
(100 pages, 2020) ISBN 978 09531 08985
is available from its publisher: shogifoundation.co.uk

From the back cover of the book:

SHAKESPEARE AS PHILOSOPHER
AND
THE SHAKESPEAREAN TRAGEDY OF EDWARD DE VERE

The two main parts of this book offer an account of 'Shakespearean' philosophy and tragic de Vere, seventeenth earl of Oxford (1550-1604). 'Shakespeare as Philosopher' highlights some of the conceptual sense or senselessness expressed in his works: in particular clarifying various dramatic and reflective themes - including of kings, war and honour - together with other scenes which show certain philosophical characters, as well as the quite clearly autobiographical Sonnets.

'The Shakespearean Tragedy of Edward de Vere' presents evidence from his early years, continental tour and a chronology of later life, especially in relation to the again evident strongly autobiographical four plays *Love's Labours Lost, As You Like It, Timon* and *Hamlet.* This book also provides a consistent determination of Shakespeare's works approximate composition dates; and outlines the period 1604-1623 with other hands to the First Folio.

It remains of interest to understand something about the actual lives of individuals behind their works - even authors of great anonymous or pseudonymous works - and not to confuse different identities. The given circumstantial strongly suggestive detailed facts, in this particular case, fit together to form a relatively clear picture: Edward de Vere is by far the most credible, compelling candidate for being William Shakespeare. This coherent and grounded identification, as the poet and playwright in question, does not simply bring in many unnecessary assumptions; the tradition of the very different contemporary man William Shakspere of Stratford-upon-Avon itself rests on a host of assumptions, which need to be reassessed without prejudice - and given the evidence (or lack of it) abandoned. A crucial distinction needs to be recognized here between 'the poet and the player'. One main question to be answered is: why did Edward de Vere not plainly state that he was William Shakespeare?

The final few pages included are of primarily 'unpoetic' philosophy, that is, objective concepts, describing individual freedom of necessity – drawing from *Oneself the Mystic and Philosopher.*

This book *Shakespeare as Philosopher and the Shakespearean Tragedy of Edward de Vere* by Tony Hosking (100 pages, 2016) ISBN 978 09531 08961 is available from its publisher: shogifoundation.co.uk